BABA

BABA

A RETURN TO CHINA UPON MY FATHER'S SHOULDERS

BELLE YANG

A HARVEST BOOK
HARCOURT BRACE & COMPANY
San Diego   New York   London

Requests for permission to make copies of any part of the work
should be mailed to: Permissions Department, Harcourt Brace & Company,
6277 Sea Harbor Drive, Orlando, Florida 32887-6777.

Library of Congress Cataloging-in-Publication Data
Yang, Belle.
Baba: a return to China upon my father's shoulders/Belle Yang.—1st ed.
p.   cm.—(A Harvest book)
ISBN 0-15-600239-6
1. China—History—20th Century—Fiction.   2. Teenage boys—China—
Fiction   3. Family—China—Fiction   I. Title.
PS3575.A53B33   1994
813'.54—dc20   94-16410

The text was set in Granjon.

Designed by Lisa Peters
Printed in the United States of America
First Harvest edition 1996
A B C D E

For Rachel Wachtel

May the stories of your people

be your spiritual fortress.

CONTENTS

In March of 1991, a friend of mine in San Francisco, Sue Yung Li, sent me a package with a scribbled note: "Thought you might enjoy reading this." Inside, she said, were photographed illustrations painted by a writer-artist named Belle Yang. Also included: a dozen pages of Belle's prose—something to read in my spare time.

I found myself in a guilt-inducing predicament, for there I was, involuntarily holding in my hands another writer's passion and dreams, a life's work that was either about to blossom or wither, depending on luck, the presence of angels, and the kindness of strangers.

Unfortunately, my reserves of kindness had long been depleted; I didn't have time to write my own work, let alone extra time to read that of a stranger. With much guilt weighing on my heart I sadly placed the young writer's unopened packet in the pile destined for The Junkmail Graveyard, otherwise known as my recycling bin.

Though I lacked kindness, I have had no lack of angels in my life. I cannot explain or describe who these angels are, only that they have showered me with a considerable amount of kindness and luck. Also, they ceaselessly remind me of this fact, which causes me to suspect they are mostly Chinese. In any case, my angels believed that I'd soon come to my senses and open Belle Yang's packet. Didn't I remember, they asked, that they had helped me in just such a way when I was an unpublished writer not so long ago? Didn't they help guide my early writing into the caring hands of writers like Amy Hempel and Molly Giles, while others might have turned my early efforts into handy strips of firestarter? In due time, the angels assured me, I'd retrieve Belle Yang's packet from the graveyard pile. I just needed to be nudged. Ever so lightly.

Over the next few days, Belle Yang's packet fell out whenever I reshuffled the pile. It surfaced to the top, no matter how many times it was buried beneath multiple copies of Victoria's Secret catalogs and sweepstakes notices. There were other hints. A cousin named Yang called.

An issue of *Belle Lettres* arrived. And then I developed an insatiable desire to hear the sound of bells, not just ordinary bells, but Chinese bells. On my desk was a pair of old copper clappers I had recently found in an antique shop. I clanged them together, and they produced a spectacularly resonant *trrrnnng!* that floated into my chest, flowed into my heart, then stubbornly lodged into that place of memory that nags at you like a universal mother asking you if you've done your homework yet. Not yet, not yet, not yet. *Trrrnnng!* You know you're going to have to do it, the angels told me.

I opened Belle's packet. Glossy photographs fell out, the illustrations Sue Yung Li had mentioned. They are stunning: splashes of watercolor creating deceptively simple images woven into vibrant patterns. The paintings are very much alive, capturing balance and disharmony between this world and the underworld, between heaven and earth, between humans and nature. They are both scary and humorous, personal and, yet, a larger view of the world. Whoever this Belle Yang is, I thought to myself, she paints well, I'll grant her that.

I then picked up the pages and began to read the vignettes of Baba, based on stories and boyhood reminiscences of Belle Yang's father. Soon I was gasping and sighing, hearing the music of Belle Yang's words, seeing and experiencing the fullness of a once-lost world she had re-created with the same vibrancy as her paintings.

In reading those few pages, I sensed the excitement veteran editors must feel when, in discovering a fresh voice, they once again find joy abundant enough to sustain them through next year's tedious editorial meetings. Belle's voice is so true and pure it is capable of washing away the grimy layers of cynicism, the dust of ennui, the greasiness of business. I felt lucky to be the recipient of her work. I called Sue Yung Li and thanked her. I called Belle and congratulated her. I called my agent and said, "I have something very, very special I think you should see."

This is *not* to say I discovered Belle Yang, for others had already discovered her writing and art before I did. But that was how I discovered once again why I love to read stories, why I once wanted to paint stories myself.

Baba is a work of twin arts. It reminds me of the earliest reason I became a writer: As a child, I wanted to be an artist. Using charcoal, pastels, and paints, I sought to capture my perceptions of the world or, rather, a precise and specific moment that conveyed what I saw, what I believed, what I *felt* was true about life that no one else could possibly understand unless I rendered it clearly and well.

I possessed more-than-average abilities in executing reasonable likenesses of still life subjects—for instance, my tabby cat, Fufu, lying on his back in the sun. Adults praised my work: "Why, that looks just like Fufu!" But I could capture none of what was more important to me. Not the differences: the intelligence of Fufu's naughtiness, for example. Nor the emotions: the twist in my heart when Fufu, lost for days, wailed to me from within a locked closet. Nor the ephemeral aspects of life's quiet intensity: how

my breath on Fufu caused his ears to flutter just like the moths that caressed our porchlight.

I always fell short of drawing what I felt, what I saw in that one magical second. And while there is enormous satisfaction in the physicality of drawing, there is a stone-in-the-throat sort of disappointment in seeing large and pitiful results before one's very eyes. Even though I swept my brush boldly across the page, even though I dabbed at details with blind patience, the right lines, colors, and shapes always eluded me. And so I eventually turned to my tools of second choice: I tried to use words to paint pictures.

Those are the reasons I admire and envy Belle Yang's double talents. She writes what she sees and feels. She draws what she sees and feels. She does so with mastery in both crafts. As Yang points out herself, in Chinese art there is no separation between pictures and words. They come from the same source. She creates painted stories, as well as story paintings. Through bold strokes of poetry and color, Yang evokes a likeness of a world now gone but retrieved through memory: the redbeard bandits, the son on a rooftop crowing instructions to the dead, the *hwwoolong* sounds of bombs landing in the marsh. She captures her own family folktales and long-standing rumors, as well as our own willingness to believe they must be true: that a prophetic dream from a goddess could foretell both judicious and unfair results, that the origins of one family's wealth came from a glowing three-legged creature that served as a divining rod to buried urns of gold.

What is equally amazing to me is the fact that Belle Yang *sees* transparently between Chinese and English. She's an American writer who writes in English and thinks in Chinese. Her writing feels Chinese to me without the awkwardness of word-for-word transliteration and without the paleness of "something lost in translation" for the sake of accessibility to the Western reader. It is as though we, the readers of English, can now miraculously read Chinese.

As an American writer who understands Chinese but speaks it like a child, I both appre-ciate and envy Belle Yang's literary feats. It is one thing to write proficiently in two languages, another to *sense* the world in two languages. By that, I mean that Belle Yang *senses* the lost world of her father in Chinese: the brusque and matter-of-fact rhythms of life, the folk imagery, the historical undertones of classical art, the noisy onomatopoeia of country and city life, the sour, appeasing, and deeply satisfying tastes of food, the adverse and harmonious relationship between humans and nature, the bitter and belly-laughing ironies, and the circular ways in which everything makes perfect if not logical sense. Yet she conveys all this with English, with poetry, with the universal power of language. She has created a world we can lose ourselves in, and when we emerge we are all the better for it. For a few lingering moments, we can even see magic in our own world. What a gift.

Baba makes me want to paint again. With watercolors, with words, whatever I can use. I want to paint the angels who urged me to see Belle Yang's work.

"SO MUCH WEARINESS . . . Fighting the water, struggling across the river Liu, carrying you pickaback, and, once reaching the sandy bank, limping, inching down the wagon roads. Daughter, it was that same dream again," Baba used to say to me. "I carried you through the dunes and across the plains of Manchuria, shouldered you into the vanished landscape of my youth; and always—always, in this dream, you are only two or three. . . ."

But today I can tell you that this dream no longer plays in the night for Baba, for during the waking hours of the past three years, my father has taken me down a meandering, tortuous road of memory. It was breathtaking and sobering to see the scope of his life's scenery.

With each segment of the journey, he would set me on his shoulders and step into a spreading landscape that in the foreground was composed of intimate, human scenes, playing out one next to another: stories unrolling in time and space like motifs of a great, long Chinese scroll. Some-times we dallied in peaceful settings; other times, we hurried away from places in the white heat of war. From my perch upon his shoulders, I saw the land, the sky, and the unfolding of events between them at the level of obscure (but not simple) lives: at the dusty level of the heart-to-heart, where men's hopes wrestle with reality.

During my journey upon Baba's shoulders, of course, he revealed himself, but oh so much more beyond himself: his focus was on the lives of the men and women we encountered, those who had painted his childhood and youth with movement and color.

In keeping company with these personalities (Uncle Zhao, the ex-bandit; Old Lady Lu, the witch doctor; Idiot Yuan, a Daoist beggar; Dong Gar, the orphan; wealthy Third Uncle; Second Brother, who was ransomed with two cows), I grasped contradictory visions, opposing views: I was enabled to see from a multiplicity of angles—in effect, I saw in the round a pocket of the past. I tasted the pungent and flavorful:

not unlike the infamous Chinese *choudoufu*—fermented tofu—with its wealth of mold, stink, and aroma, eaten hot and spicy with red pepper and garlic.

It was with the unpolished, fragmentary knowledge of the child that I made my return upon Baba's shoulders (I could have had no better guide to history, for Baba is a great reader, an observer, a man of memory and insight); but as we ambled down in time from the fading days of the Qing dynasty, through the Japanese invasion of Manchuria, the onslaught of the Russians after the defeat of the Japanese, and the ensuing civil war, my senses were progressively honed keener—my awareness growing broader—all the better to understand the profound events that would bring forth an ideology that eventually submerged everything in its path.

Stepping back in time, Baba had to relive the circumstances; to shoulder me into the landscape, it was necessary for him to endure once again the bittersweet ironies but also to embrace the beauty, joy, and wisdom of a world now lost. (I know that on nights after we had returned from a sally into the past, Baba had trouble falling asleep: it was easy to call fierce emotions into the present but difficult to unloose them back into forgetfulness.)

After each venture into a segment of that landscape, we were able to step forth into the haven of the present, to breathe and to rest. Each time we emerged, Baba was ready to surrender past sorrows and disappointments to present anecdotes, humor, and, above all, laughter. But more important, upon each of our returns, Baba's burden was lightened: he felt a joy in having fulfilled his duty to mark the poignant passage of quiet folk—men like the luckless hired hand Uncle Yu.

But let me return to a time before our journey. I must tell you we had no natural understanding, Baba and I: his spiritual address was in the East, mine so much in the West.

My preparation for the entry into the land-

scape (though at the time I did not know it to be a preparation; it felt to me like a disquieting severance from the familiar). It took the form of a physical return to China. For one like myself, planted in the hospitable American soil early in life, it was necessary to return to the rawness of origin, to learn the symbols, the codes, the iconography, that would serve me as keys with which to unlock Baba's memories. It took a full embrace of the written and the spoken Chinese, for in order to reach a truly deep understanding of him, I had to tap into the original language in which his ideas were given form. Only then could I ask the questions that would stir him enough to carry me into the past.

In the fall of 1986, I flew to Beijing (as of this writing, six years ago to the day) to study classical Chinese art, focusing on the great tradition of landscape painting—an art of time as well as space. I learned to cast away Western perspective and vault into the sky like the Monkey King of legend—to see the world from a multiplicity of angles (the Chinese landscape is intensely different from a Western one, where the viewer remains, still as a rock, at one fixed point).

In my study and practice of this art—this philosophy, this way of life—I grew more convinced of what I had always felt, what I had always seen in Baba's art and poetry: that there is no separation of words and images. For in Chinese painting, the words—the artist's reflections—are integral to the painting; the images, integral to the words: both of them drawn from the same immeasurable, ever-replenishing source.

During my years of study, I roamed across the land, sketching, painting, looking. I reached regions closed to foreigners, to which my yellow skin gained me easy (though, admittedly, nervous) entry. I traveled the Gobi Desert along the Silk Road, where Buddhism first made its appearance in the Middle Kingdom; I dug into the yellow earth of the Great Northwest and laid my hands upon pottery, art of the late Stone Age, fitting my fingers into the clay imprints of hands left by craftsmen of some seven thousand years ago; I returned to the frozen Manchurian north to celebrate Spring Festival, the Chinese New Year, with my grandparents, whose heads were frosted white with layers of remembrance; I submerged myself in the Hunan countryside of the Miao tribes, where the only "foreigners" seen previously were travelers from a neighboring county.

In my wanderings across a land of vastly different temperaments, my eyes were opened to a wealth of folk art, the cultural antithesis of the lofty, scholarly classical Chinese painting I had come to study (though their final aims are the same: to stir the heart). My heart was moved by the paper cuts, the vibrant graphics of the New Year prints, the naïf paintings of the peasants, each region stylistically distinct. These were works of men and women deeply rooted in their soil; works populated with farm animals, fruits of the field and stream; they were celebrations of birth, marriage, harvest, the seasons, Heaven and Earth, youth, old age, and death. The art of the countryfolk swelled with candor and humor; in their very artlessness they captured life more directly than any attempt at careful imitation could ever do.

In the spring of my third year in China, the energy I had sensed upon arrival, an underlying tension, a raw nervousness, a fluttering excitement, stirring below the surface of the society, emerged and manifested itself in heady days of hope and optimism. New ideas had brought vigor—most pronounced in the cities; fresh ideas were surging from across the seas; suppressed ideas welled up from belowground. I felt as if every day I would awaken to amazing changes. And I was as excited as anyone. As time progressed, the energy grew wilder, the voices of the people grew louder, culminating in the passions of "Democracy Spring." But I saw it quelled. Brutally. And in the aftermath of June 4, 1989, I saw books burned, stories destroyed. I saw artists frightened and numbed into silence. Great cultures tell life-sustaining stories, but in China, small lies choked the air.

Physically depleted, in spiritual exhaustion, I returned to America late in 1989, but I returned with gratitude in my heart for the freedom of expression given me in America. I returned convinced that I would firmly grasp that generous gift with both hands—always.

This conviction has resulted in the telling, in my own fashion, of the story that I, the daughter of Joseph Yang, have learned to love. It is the story of Baba—he who talks for a long, long chain of others: the voiceless, the overlooked; those who have disappeared in the tumult of time without a murmur. And it has resulted in the painting of this peopled landscape that unrolls at your feet—a landscape that I hope you will choose to enter.

BELLE YANG

On this sixtieth birthday of my mother,
September 8, 1992
Carmel, California

BABA

IN A TIME WHEN the world was a bit wider, during a season when the sorghum was tinged with red, Baba journeyed the lonely sixty li from the town of Xinmin on a horse-drawn wagon for a visit with kinfolk in Shantuozi, deep in the countryside. The steady *quok-quok-quok* of the animal's hooves and an occasional "Jiaaah!" from the driver, urging the nag on, were the only sounds threading through the fields of murmuring sorghum that unrolled into the Manchurian horizon.

The land was generous: this was the fertile black-soil belt of China.

And jogged into half-dreams upon the wagon under the big sky, Baba envisioned, from tales passed down to him, how the Great Progenitor of the Yang Clan had ferried his wife, his two small sons, and all their worldly possessions—their pots and pans—upon the platform of a squeaky wheelbarrow, and how they had arrived in this land during the last decade of the eighteenth century.

It was during this age that the rule of the Manchus in the capital, Beijing, whose ancestors were nomads upon these great northeastern plains, was entering its tottering, feeble years of decay and could no longer bar the Chinese from settling upon this, their sacred homeland.

The Great Progenitor—whose face Baba imagined was as austerely handsome as that of the Patriarch, his grandfather—had come to claim a patch of this land known as Manchuria, which bordered upon Mongolia, Siberia, Korea, the Yellow Sea. Here, he and his family would escape the grip of hunger that lay in other regions of the Middle Kingdom. Here, his children and theirs would grow into tall, big-boned men and women, doing honor to the land and sky that did not contain them but allowed them to swing their limbs, take lavish strides.

"Jiaaah!" The wagoner's voice again ripped into the air and lingered.

At dusk, Baba spied Old Granddaddy Hill in the distance, silhouetted against the scarlet sky, and saw the crows returning to roost in the cypresses that crowned the hill, under whose layers of shadows generations of his ancestors lay in eternal rest; at this sight, his heart was cheered by the thought that he would soon be under a kind, familiar roof.

And upon arrival, he was not disappointed. As always, he was embraced by warm smiles, given a hot meal, then curled up upon a kang, a brick platform topped with rush mats, hollow underneath to allow the circulation of hot air piped in from the kitchen stove.

On some nights, if he felt so inclined, Baba joined three cousins under the cover of a breezy shack that was thrust high into the sky by four thick willow posts; from this aerie, the boys kept watch for thieves over the field of ripening watermelons. When it rained, it was wonderful to listen to the *stk, stk* of the raindrops as they hurtled against the thatching; but as the boys lay toasty warm on their bed of sweet hay, the rain soon leaked through and splashed down upon their nest.

Sometimes they heard the wolves howl and scamper about just outside the sorghum that grew around the perimeter of the melon field. The cousins were familiar with the sounds, but Baba, a boy from the city of Xinmin—whose branch of the ever-growing clan had struck out on its own away from Shantuozi—was terrified by the snuffling, the quick succession of crunching footsteps in the sandy soil, and the shadows bent to the ground, sniffing, creeping toward them. A three-foot-wide trench, six feet deep, ringed the field and deterred the groundhogs from chewing on the melons—they fell in and were snared by tiny nooses fashioned from willow switches—but the wolves easily traversed the trough. This was the reason for the four lengthy posts beneath the hut.

The wolves were most active at night but were also a menace during the day. In the summer, when there were many small mammals scurrying about, they hunted singly or ranged in small groups; but in the winter, when rodents, hares, birds became scarce, the wolves hunted bigger animals, making forays in large packs out of the groves of dense, scrubby willows that grew along the banks of the Liu. When ravenous, and so made bold, they attacked the soulful little donkeys with white eye rings and long, feathery lashes, the kind loved by northerners—not speedy, but agile, with a streak of stubbornness not unlike that coursing through the blood of the Manchurians themselves. The wolves bit the donkeys' shanks and nipped at their throats, while the drivers snapped their whips at the harness bells to set them jangling; the sudden noise sent the scoundrels scuttling. If a man journeyed alone and on foot in the winter, he would set dry brown fields ablaze to fend off the four-legged assailants.

Because of the threat of wolves, Baba and all the children were admonished not to wander along the banks of the Liu: for once when Widow Sun had waited long past the dinner hour for her son, the next day the villagers found bits of a child's rib cage strewn in a clearing, along the bank where the little one had been tending goats.

When Baba first came upon Widow Sun in Shantuozi, she was already quite old. The villagers respectfully called her Sun Da Nainai— Old Grandmother Sun—though she could never claim a grandchild of her very own. In the summertime, at dusk, she could often be found in a field of tall sorghum, separating the tassels of the plants that had become entangled in the breeze. "Now quit this foolin'! Why must y'all fight among yourselves," Baba heard her scold. After Old Grandmother Sun lost her husband and her only child, she lost her mind, and became a *yaofan*—one who asks for rice.

Now, you must know that subjects of the Middle Kingdom are a people intensely preoccupied with the state of the stomach—more so, I am prone to believe, than any other folk to inhabit this earth. The standard greeting is: *'Ni chi le ma?'*—Have you eaten?—which, with no intention of inviting the other person to dinner (nor does the one thus greeted harbor any illusion of having been invited), simply means: "How are you?" The anticipated response to this salutation

is a hearty: *"Chi guo le, chi guo le"*—Yes, yes, I've eaten.

But when Old Grandmother Sun made her yearly visit to the various households, her fellow villagers generously filled her grain sacks; they expected her and greeted her as an old friend. *"Ni chi le ma?"* they would say; and in her case it was a genuine invitation, not a hollow "hello." They set out an extra bowl and a pair of chopsticks for her at the dinner table.

In addition to the menace of the wolves, Baba was warned about the highwaymen—fellows who disdained honest labor on the land. The bandits jumped out of murky hiding places by the roadside and smashed the skulls of solitary passersby. They pocketed what was not theirs and fled. When these men grew in number, they ran in packs and raided the villages, looking for bigger prey. These better-organized bandits, known as "redbeards," rode in under various banners, but they, too, plundered and fled.

But in the years when Baba's limbs were still lengthening and his vision was ever widening, a new breed of men would come howling across the great plains; these had the biggest appetite of all: they killed, plundered, and stayed. This new breed would engorge an old, familiar way of life and send Baba, my father, wandering down the length of the Middle Kingdom, and my grandparents wandering as *yaofan* down the village roads.

Nainai, my grandmother, and her sister-in-law would travel the same roads, make the same rounds with grain sacks, as Old Grandmother Sun had done years and years before. Perhaps they would follow in the widow's footsteps in the fall, when the sorghum had ripened, or maybe they would travel earlier in the year, past unplanted fields canopied by tiny starlike yellow blossoms as far as the eye could see. But I hope they would not have to journey forth into the Manchurian winter, when the ground is frozen to the core. Nainai's sister-in-law, who was rather a jolly, oblivious sort, would sing country ditties to her as they trudged from village to village.

Yeye, my grandfather, would sometimes accompany Nainai, but he would be a surly partner: the pampered eldest son of the Patriarch, a big landowner, he would deem his back too brittle and his heart too proud to allow him to beg. He would stop outside the wattled garden gates, lean on his staff, and wait for his sweet-tempered wife to return with a little rice, a little millet, or perhaps a handful of soybeans.

In the early 1960s, there would come a great man-made famine in the Middle Kingdom, and all its subjects would be brought down to become *yaofan;* but there would be no more rice to be begged (did the folks still greet one another with the cruel words: *"Ni chi le ma?"* I have often wondered). During those years, the people would feel the hunger so keenly, they would hunt the hunters. The population of wolves would be decimated.

These tales of begging and famine young Baba and his cousins did not yet know as they listened to the rain striking the sand and the melons in the darkness of a summer's eve. But they would experience them soon enough.

These and many others are the stories that he now tells as he shoulders this thirty-year-old daughter of his, like a child of three, into his memories.

THE MEMORIES OF my father come into focus in 1931, when he was the age of three—when Baba's awareness was coaxed into the world, not by the soft clapping of the leaves of the poplar (the tree whose name, *yang,* our family assumed), but by a deafening *hwwoolong!* It was with this *hwwoolong!* that a Japanese bomb landed south of the Western Marsh, whose banks bordered upon the property of the wealthy House of Yang.

Nainai, my grandmother, was drying Baba's wet quilted trousers over the brazier. The glass windowpanes inhaled and exhaled, but the paper panes heaved a sigh and suddenly gave way, cracking like white porcelain.

Nainai, pregnant with her fifth child, ran out of the house with Baba in tow, his bare bottom cruelly exposed to the November bite. Down the craw and into the maw of the subterranean storage space they tumbled. In the gloom, it was hard to distinguish the heads of cabbages from the heads of the members of the House of Yang:

the Patriarch and the Matriarch, Baba's grandparents; innumerable uncles, aunts, cousins; and his three elder brothers. His father was not to be found among the relatives and the assorted vegetables; working in the center of town for the warlord government of Zhang Xueliang, he had been evacuated with other civil servants as the government fled from the advancing Japanese.

After the danger had passed, the family emerged from the storage space, blinking in the light, giving off an odor of turnips.

The Japanese pilots had seen the south-fleeing Chinese military encamped on the Yang property and had targeted the family's roof. But the bomb had wavered and drifted, carried southwest by strong winds.

The unlucky recipient of the stray bomb was none other than the Xiao family. The folk of Xinmin referred to each man, woman, and child of the Xiao clan, without distinction—as Baba would later learn to do—by the divine title Xiao Dafen—Xiao the Dung Patty. It was no denigration; it was their rightful epithet, for the Xiao family trade was the manufacture of fertilizer. When Baba was of school age, he would not see any of the juvenile "Patties" among his classmates when he went to school: the truants helped in the gathering of animal and human excrement, which would be mixed with sand, earth, and water in a deep pit. Their ancestors had been in the manure business, and doubtless the future generations of Xiaos would carry on in this life-giving, life-enhancing industry.

The family of seven—all of the same mold: short, round, and squat—were later found to be frightened but safe. The barnlike structure that was their home remained leaning at its usual chancy angle, but the smooth field, the size of a basketball court, where the Xiaos methodically, and with antlike steadfastness, spooned out neat rows of the pie-size patties of manure to bake in the sun, this field was pocked by a crater two feet deep and six feet wide. At least a half-dozen patties were launched heavenward, landing Lord knows where.

As the Japanese bombers flew southward toward Jinzhou, it was later told, many a peasant in the field had squinted up at the sky while exclaiming:

"Well, look at that! More big locusts buzzing way up yonder."

In the recent past, the countryfolk had often watched, in astonished silence, the maneuvers of the one-engine, Italian-make airplanes belonging to the fleet of Warlord Zhang; how were these giant insects able to cling to the sky? they had wondered. In their brief acquaintance with the flying machines, they had not known one to drop objects from the sky. But this was just what those directly above their heads were now observed doing. As the attacking Japanese flew over Xinmin, Baba's hometown, the men and womenfolk below stood drop-jawed, pointing at the enemy planes, saying: "Well, look at that! The big insects are dropping bottles . . . bottles, of all things!"

When the bottles landed in their pigsties and flung their animals to swine heaven, knowledge exploded upon them.

In all the neighborhoods, the Zhaos, the Wangs, the Wus, the Huangs, were talking about the destruction dealt by the bottles. They had an understanding of bullets—that they were capable of putting holes in a man—but they had never witnessed a force capable of tearing off the hind leg of a cow . . . leg of a cow! A cow was the most massive thing in existence. The more they talked, the more fearful they became. Xinmin was in an uproar.

But in a short time, folk throughout the Manchurian countryside learned to shield themselves from the falling bottles; when the *woong-woong-woong* of the big insects sounded overhead, they knew better than to stand and gape; some ran with wooden tables upon their backs to ward off the blows.

What a strange new world;
Suddenly a big locust demon in the sky.
It devours the wheat in the fields;
It is also hungry for our little lives.
The farmers throw down their hoes and hide;
"The dawn of a new age!" they cry.

This was the brand-new ditty the older children were belting out. Baba, too, was mouthing the words, tasting them upon his tongue, exploring their shapes, separated from their significance. With the Japanese invasion of Manchuria, which had commenced at midnight on September 18, 1931, this new tune had become the song of the land.

In no time, the bottles from the sky had subdued the inhabitants of Manchuria, now to become the Japanese puppet state Manchukuo. A descendant of the fallen Qing dynasty was picked up by the scruff, helpless and mewing, and deposited on the throne as emperor.

In the immediate years after the Japanese takeover, Baba would often see a human curio come sip jasmine tea with the Patriarch. Because he was a relation, however distant (the Patriarch's great-grandfather's cousin's fifth daughter-in-law's somebody or other!), he was welcomed like family.

"Ah, this is as it should be," he would say

to Baba's stately grandfather. "How can the Earth hold steady without the Emperor? The Dragon Throne has been empty for the last two decades." He was known as Wang the Imperial Scholar to all, though in his numerous tries, he had never managed to pass even the lowest of the imperial examinations during the time of the last dynasty. But because he was crowned with such a weighty title early on, he felt duty bound to live up to it. Practice became habit, and over the years, he came to move at a steady, unflustered gait—no, an imperial scholar should never be seen to bounce around town, allowing his gown to flap wildly. Yet his ancient eyes—the pupils blue-gray with cataracts—were still suffused with a befogged innocence.

Scholar Wang wore a Manchu skullcap decorated with a large red pompon at the crown, and he draped his body with a neat dark gown, but this was not what attracted attention among those who had adopted the Western suit. What made him eccentrically old-fashioned was the manner in which he wore his hair.

As an assertion of his loyalty to the fallen Qing dynasty, the old man had maintained his very skinny pigtail, which fell all the way down to his tailbone. Most everyone else had, ages ago, cut off the queue that symbolized the subservience of the Han Chinese to the alien ruling Manchus—nomads who had galloped in from the grasslands. At the end of his braid, using bright red string, Scholar Wang dangled two coins from the Qianlong reign, the glory days of Manchu rule.

"My old friend," he would say to the perfectly proper Patriarch, who collected poets, artists, mystics, and others prone to deviate from the general flow, "as you well know, it's been over twenty years since the overthrow of the Qing dynasty. In this time, the people have eaten nothing but bitterness. The warlords, they stick those silly feather dusters atop their hats—what do you call 'em . . . ah, the shakos—after the style of the European military and strut about. They fight one another for control of the land. They tear the Middle Kingdom apart, limb by limb.

"And there are those who talk of a republican form of government. What nonsense! We need to return to the old, time-tested way, the venerable Confucian order. . . .

"The astrologers say they have seen the purple light over Beiping drift north toward Changchun, the new imperial residence," said he, his elegant fingers curled around the teacup. "There will be peace, now that the Son of Heaven has been restored."

When Baba was old enough to know embarrassment, he would say to himself upon seeing on the street this man whose thin pigtail swung sedately with the weight of the coins: "I know he's kin and all, but I do wish he would not come over to our house. Not so often at least." He would study the man out of the corner of his eyes, watching him shift his old legs in a measured pace under his stiff gown—a man who took it upon himself to maintain the pillarlike stance of one who stood as a milestone to the past.

It was Wang the Imperial Scholar's good fortune to die before the fall of the last emperor, when the Japanese surrendered Manchuria, following the detonation of atomic bottles over Hiroshima and Nagasaki.

But that would come much later. For the time being, the Japanese were in Manchuria to stay, and they were looking farther south, to the other choice parts of the Middle Kingdom, though this was not even a rumor to three-year-old Baba.

My father's horizon, which for the moment had advanced only to the garden gate, would very soon make a great, abrupt leap outward.

THE ONSLAUGHT OF the Japanese on Manchuria had severed Yeye, my grandfather, from the family; he had been swept along with the warlord government to south of the Great Wall, into the protective embrace of China proper.

Over two years later, in the summer of 1934, when an unofficial truce teetered between the Chinese and the Japanese, the Patriarch, my great-grandfather, escorted Nainai and her five children—now including a year-old girl, whom Yeye had never laid eyes upon—to Tianjin for a reunion. The Patriarch returned to Manchuria, the House of Yang being still intact and prospering; the Japanese occupiers, though their entry had been brutal, did not wish to disrupt further the life pulse of the people. They manipulated quietly behind the scenes through the puppet emperor.

"I want to go back," six-year-old Baba blurted upon arrival at their new home in Tianjin. Through a veil of tears, he watched his

mother set up the altar of Guanyin, the Goddess of Mercy, light three sticks of incense, as thick as his own small fingers, then kowtow three times. Homage to Guanyin was Nainai's first order of business following a move to a new place.

"There's not much we can do, Number Four. Manchuria is under occupation. We're better off here in Tianjin for the time being, and besides, your father really enjoys his new work as the general manager of Jingjing Coal Mining Company," Nainai said. Her high forehead was as smooth and untroubled as that of the goddess.

The foot-high bronze Guanyin rested upon the petals of an unfolding lotus; the ancient sun symbol, the swastika (derived from the Sanskrit *svasti*—well-being) lay at the base of her throat. Her demure eyes were cast downward, but Nainai knew the deity would watch over her family; she would grant all entreaties born of a genuine heart.

At night, Baba lay awake, listening for the

plaintive whistle of the train bound for the north, his fledgling soul traveling home with the locomotive to the great plains, to the South Garden, to the animals in the yard.

But within a year's time, Baba's longings had been diluted: he had grown accustomed to life in Tianjin, had come to love the noise and commotions of the port city. With a bread roll stuffed inside his pocket, he wandered freely into the different quarters.

For Yeye's convenience, the family had settled on the eastern bank of the river Hai, in a section of the city called Dawangzhuang—Big Village of the Wang Clan: here, he was just a stroll away from his riverside office.

Crossing over on the drawbridge, Wanguoqiao—the Bridge of Ten Thousand Nations—Baba was able to reach the foreign concessions, canopied by an exuberance of trees.

He found the French concession—Lizhan Boulevard in particular, with its many shops, theaters, and restaurants—"hot and noisy," fe-

vered with activities, stirring with fragrances. It was policed by agile Vietnamese sporting berets, their teeth stained black from chewing betel nuts.

The British concession, where the family had initially planned to take up residence, was subdued by comparison to the French; as Baba wandered residential London Street, lined with stately lamps, he was greeted by the soft talk of a piano or the mispronunciations of a child on the violin. Indian guards, wearing white turbans that looked like swelling *mantou*—Chinese steamed bread—and displaying king-size beards (they sprouted more facial hair than the combined growth of Baba's father and uncles), maintained order.

The Italian and the Japanese concessions were dimmed by the radiance of their more prosperous neighbors; wealthy Chinese avoided these concessions and chose to nest in the luxury of the French and British.

The Russians were the shabbiest among the foreigners, Baba concluded. They had lost their concession after the Russian Revolution and now resided in a row of houses on a wide boulevard among the Chinese in Dawangzhuang.

"I've seen them before—red faces, great big green eyes, flaring nostrils, and golden fur: the horrible statues in the Demon Temple!" said Baba when he first spied a Russian "foreign devil."

In the summertime, the Russians dragged dining tables and chairs outside their houses and caroused, dancing on the sidewalk; the night air hung with the crescendo of their lusty voices, the smell of alcohol, the flight of silver moths.

These were the White Russians, the exiles, the minor aristocrats who lived off the proceeds of the sale of jewelry and other family heirlooms. When they had sold everything—down to the last glass bead—they sought employment as bodyguards, domestics, or dance hall hostesses; asked what their occupation was, "prince" or "princess" was often the reply.

But the Russians were most notable for their prescience; they were hair-trigger sensitive to changes in the political climate and thus acutely aware of the approach of danger. Suddenly one year, Baba saw that the row of Russian houses in Dawangzhuang had come to resemble an empty pea pod. There were no more sounds of scraping table and chair legs on the sidewalk on summer eves. Where had they all gone to? Most of the occupants had spilled south to Shanghai.

In that same year—when Baba turned eight—days before grain was to be harvested in the countryside, he stood watching the sky over Tianjin darken, fear mounting in his chest. Soon the city was mantled by clouds of locusts so dense, they quenched the summer sun. The air motored with the *woong-woong-woong* of their cellophane wings. "*Wanle! Wanle!*—It's all over! It's all over for the farmers!" Baba heard the grown-ups crying to Heaven in resignation, their hands raised. Within two hours, little was left of the crops in the countryside.

Now that the locusts had consumed the people's grain, the people would fill their bellies with locusts—enormous, obscene locusts, four inches long, with large, slanting, contentious eyes. (Countryfolk named them *qingtouleng*— green lunkheads—for their village-idiot stares. The term *qingtouleng* was often applied to foolhardy youths.)

Soon the peasants came to the city to peddle the live insects, teeming in enormous covered baskets. Ranging into neighbors' homes, Baba watched the Tianjin cooks pluck off the wings and hind legs one by one; the insects, missing these appendages, reared their tails; the poor things resembled oversize cashews as they maneuvered on their remaining four legs. Hundreds of them, crawling over one another in white enamel basins in the kitchens, awaited death in the sizzling wok. They were fried *en masse* in oil, until golden crisp and fragrant like pastry crust. Females with eggs were especially savory.

But it was not a fair trade, grain for locusts. There was hunger. Food prices soared. Baba saw beggars selling sons and daughters on the streets. One day, he watched the performance of a rag-ged man who pounded upon a drum made from a long section of thick bamboo, a piece of skin stretched over one end; copper coins tied with wires to the side of the drum jangled with a melancholic *ching-ching-ching*. As the man made music, his son danced like a trained animal, stood on his hands and, with great agility, sprang back onto his feet. Baba looked deep into the intelligent eyes of the boy, who was his own age and was very nice-looking beneath the dust on his face and the tattered clothing. He felt sorry for the boy. Whenever the pair was favored with a few coppers by a passerby, the father and son bowed deeply and neatly to their benefactor.

"Soon there will be pestilence even more devastating than the locusts," Baba heard people say that year.

Now the Japanese had been in Manchuria for nearly six years, but they were not satisfied solely with ingesting the northeast. Their appetite had been whetted, and they fixed their gaze upon Hebei Province, which lay just south of the Great Wall. They claimed that this territory was necessary to Manchuria as a buffer against the Chinese to the south. Tianjin lay in Hebei Province.

As the Japanese contingent from Manchuria marched on Tianjin, pairs of Chinese soldiers in gray uniforms appeared in the narrow alleys. Baba thought it strange. Their swords, with flamboyant, flaring blades and handles wrapped with blue and white ribbons, looked like the weapons flashed in mock battle scenes in Chinese operas.

"Who ordered the soldiers here? And did they really think such weaponry would be effective against the enemy?" the grown-ups wondered out loud. The Japanese were equipped with the most advanced armaments then available. But before the Japanese ever reached the city, the soldiers disappeared.

On July 7, 1937 (considered by some historians as the day the Second World War began in the Far East), no more than eighty miles to the northwest of Tianjin, Japanese troops clashed with Chinese army units near the Marco Polo Bridge, just west of Beiping—Northern Peace (known prior to 1926 as Beijing—Northern Capital). Within three days, the Japanese overran the former capital itself.

But in Tianjin, news of the incursion did not wrinkle the city's surface calm. The populace did not display any signs of fear; in fact, they displayed no emotion at all. They had experienced all possible combinations of natural and man-made disasters since the latter days of the Qing dynasty. *"Meifazi*—it's out of our hands," they said with a shrug. They felt stripped of their legs and wings like the locusts.

On the day that the Japanese entered Tianjin—on foot, astride horses, riding in tanks, and hauling cannons on horse-drawn carts—its citizens gave no resistance. Baba joined the throngs, squeezing between the bodies to gawk as if at a procession of acrobats come to town on animals.

"How interesting," he said to himself. "The banners they bear on their vehicles have a bright-red dot against an all-white background. Like a domino piece. So very, very simple." It was Baba's first sighting of Japan's national flag, the rising sun.

But one cloudless, crystalline summer afternoon toward the end of July, a couple of weeks following the entrance of the Japanese into the city, Baba watched the shadows of winged machines skim across the streets of Dawangzhuang and cross over to the other side of the river. Upon reaching the northern bank, each airplane released two bombs. Because the Chinese government would not capitulate by relinquishing the province, the Japanese were escalating the war, dealing death blows to the vital organs. If Beiping was the brain, Tianjin was the heart of the province.

From Dawangzhuang, Baba and the children of the neighborhood watched with increasing horror as plumes of smoke rose from the ravaged government buildings; they breathed the acrid smell of annihilation.

The bombings had finally roused the populace from their stupor. At home, Baba heard the panicked footsteps of the grown-ups, going every which way. In the confusion, the newest addition to the family, his baby brother, disappeared in the arms of the peasant woman who had been hired to nurse him. Yeye, taking Baba's sister and his third brother with him, arranged housing on London Street in the British concession; they would be safe there, for the Japanese were careful to avoid damaging the properties of foreigners.

Nainai stayed behind to protect the house from looters. Baba and his second brother chose to remain with their mother (Eldest Brother was away, studying in Beiping): neither one of them relished the thought of passing time with their authoritarian father, who criticized their every move and struck them violently with whatever was at hand, including heavy teak furniture.

When Yeye had not returned by the second day to retrieve the rest of the family, Nainai sent Baba and his second brother to seek refuge on the waterfront.

"Get! Go on. Go on, you two," she said with

firmness, pressing money for food into their hands. "Go to one of the warehouses that fly foreign flags. The Japanese won't dare drop their bombs on those places," said she. "I'll still need to stay on and watch over the house. Those looters are getting more aggressive, breaking into abandoned houses in broad daylight now."

When they arrived at the waterfront warehouse of Butterfield and Swire, the British trading company, they found its environs teeming with refugees. The two boys found shelter under the enormous roof, in among the filth generated by a mass of bodies. They had no choice but to remain inside, for by nightfall the Japanese had imposed martial law on the city. But within the vast facility, Baba and his brother were quickly separated, lost in the chaos of the tens of thousands of refugees. To add to the tension, a storm pummeled the city that night. The rain beat down on the river. The rain drummed on the tin roof.

The next day, and the next, the rain clattered down like never-ending applause. Inside the dim warehouse, Baba heard rumors that fishermen on the river had in recent weeks been pulling up hefty fish the size of carp—but as bright as goldfish. "This is queer! Never seen such before—these blood-colored fish," people said. "What craziness! Must be an omen of bad things to come. . . ."

At night, he tried to scrunch down among the strangers, the monotonous sound of the rain dulling his mind. He closed his eyes and tried to sleep, yet could not, his thoughts drifting to his mother, a solitary woman defending a darkened house.

He was close to her, as were all his siblings. A gentle soul, she rarely uttered a mean word in wrath. If she found him filching string for his kite from her sewing box, she reached very slowly for her short broom, allowing him plenty of time to make his escape. Once he had skedaddled, she quickly forgot his trespass.

When they were living in Manchuria, and he was still very young, he was fond of toddling after her into the North Garden, to pick cabbage for dinner. One day, he remembered, there between the rows of vegetables, two sparrows, oblivious to human company in their noisy sparring, were captured by Nainai in her generous blue-and-white print apron. She tied one bird's leg to a leg of the other with a length of string and allowed Baba to play with them for a short while; soon she came to untie the string, letting them fly free, the two birds no longer in a mood to bicker.

And it was also she who spent months painstakingly stitching cloth shoes for him to wear during Spring Festival, the Chinese New Year, when children were to have new clothes. He saw her cradling the makings of a shoe in one hand, needle and thread in the other. He remembered how she had tried to cram his foot into one of them, pounding on the sole to make it fit; but once the foot was in, the big toe was crooked inside. She was always slow to anger, but oh, the tears of frustration when she realized that her son had outgrown the shoes before she even finished stitching down the soles!

How tirelessly she worked! But her only indulgence was to puff slowly, meditatively, on her long-stemmed pipe, her face smoothing into a blank. (She had been smoking since the age of three! Pipe smoking was a common habit of Manchurian women.) And only a special kind of tobacco would do. Yeye had tried to persuade her to switch to more sophisticated-looking cigarettes, for now that he was the general manager of a big company in a modern city, a wife with a pipe was too provincial.

"Bah! This tastes bad," she had said of the cigarettes. No, she would not give up her pipe; as a harried mother and wife, she had to be allowed some small pleasure in the day.

He thought of these and many things as he squatted amid the dank bodies in the warehouse, and he decided he would go back to Nainai, peril or no peril. Where she was, that's where home was.

On the third morning, still unable to locate Second Brother in the masses, Baba made his return.

The streets were silent, becoming emptier the farther he ventured from the haven on the waterfront. The rain was now a fine mist. His own footsteps crunched too loudly in his ears. Up ahead, he saw a row of ragged men marching in single file, who, curiously enough, were directed by another filthy man, carrying a baton. Baba realized that they were a troop of opium addicts turned looters; their leader was steering them toward abandoned houses.

Farther along, Baba saw several bodies slumped in the gutters—dead bodies—and he strangled a cry; perhaps the Japanese soldiers had yelled, *"Tomale! Wugokuna!"* but the men did not respond to the orders to halt and were shot in the night.

He hugged the wall along the street, trying to slip past the Japanese soldiers at one of the many checkpoints. But they saw him. Six approached, carrying their bayonets with the blades pointed at him. Baba shrank back, pale.

"Hunnh!" one soldier cried as he made a stab at him. Clenching his stomach, Baba shut his eyes tight, but he could still see the gleam of the blade. He felt the point catch on his shirt, heard laughter. When he opened his eyes, one of the soldiers reached out for him—and rumpled his hair. They roared at their own grisly joke, enjoyed the look of terror upon the child's face. They waved him on.

Arriving at the front gate of his house, Baba, try as he might, could not push open the battered door, scarred by what looked like the repeated thrusts of bayonets. He looked wildly about.

"Mama! Mama!" he croaked, and pummeled the door with his small, impotent fists. There was no reply.

"Mama! Mama!" Misery was in his cries.

It seemed an eternity before his mother answered. Frail and distant, her worried voice sounded behind the wall. Baba nearly wept for joy.

"I can't open the gate now; I've blocked the entrance," he heard her say. "Go back! Go back to the waterfront! You'll be safer there. Here's more money for food!"

A thick roll of bills, tied with a string, landed with a gentle thud at the base of the wall. "Go back! Go back! Soldiers . . . Japanese soldiers broke in last night. . . ."

Nainai, my grandmother, then still young, fair-skinned, and lovely, had crouched in the darkness of the house on the second night of her solitary watch. Suddenly: *Boom! Boom! Boom! Boom! Boom!* She heard giants at the door.

Terror-stricken, she kowtowed before Guanyin, the Goddess of Mercy, striking her forehead on the floor as the unseen beings pounded upon the door. The cold rasp of metal upon metal. A sudden crash. The giants had come to feast.

But they were not giants; they were the "small devils," the Chinese pejorative for the Japanese.

Nainai, kneeling before Guanyin, did not dare move; she hardly dared to breathe.

"Emituofuo, emituofuo, emituofuo," she prayed in silence to Guanyin.

She heard sharp footsteps thudding in her ears and looked up in time to see a soldier raise his hand and bring his arm swinging downward. Her heart bobbed and pressed into her throat.

The sergeant doffed his cap.

He bowed deeply before the altar of Guanyin. Three of his men followed his example.

Nainai breathed. They must be praying for their wives, children, and old parents at home, she thought.

The Japanese searched throughout the house, looking for concealed Chinese soldiers, and when they had not turned up any, the sergeant nodded toward Nainai, the way a satisfied guest would acknowledge the hospitality of his hostess. Without a word, he led his men out of the house and through the front yard. Courteously, they closed the limping gate behind them.

Nainai moved quickly to pile heavy furniture against the gate from the inside. The immediate threat of the Japanese had passed, but now she feared the opium addicts looting homes in rabid bands. She heard these desperate men banging on the gate many a time during the night, heard the shrill whistles of the Japanese soldiers giving chase—sometimes the sound of gunfire—and then the receding patter of footsteps in the rain.

The midnight encounter with the Japanese soldiers had frightened my grandmother, but the men had done her no harm; nor had they rifled through chests, taken money, jewelry, and watches, as they did in the neighbors' homes.

Over the course of the week, the family members were reunited in a house at the British concession that belonged to a colleague of Yeye. The Japanese installed their puppets in the Tianjin government, and their military maneuvered south. Life in the city, on the surface, reverted to what it had been. The only noticeable difference was the little Japanese flags with which the citizens were forced to decorate the entrances to their homes.

Thenceforth, Nainai became an even more fervent believer in Guanyin's protective powers. Lighting the incense and performing her kowtows once in the morning and once at night was no longer enough: Baba also watched his mother pay homage to Guanyin at high noon.

The goddess would watch over the family wherever it moved, eventually taking everyone safely home to Manchuria.

Upon arrival in Tianjin, the Japanese expropriated the Jingjing Coal Mining Company; Yeye, my grandfather, lost his position. In that fall of 1937, he moved the family to Beiping and invested in a gold mine in the mountains of Miyun, just north of the city. But two years later, this business was also seized by the Japanese, and Yeye, for lack of better ideas, decided to return the family to Manchuria, to the patriarchal home.

Manchuria was still under Japanese occupation, and Yeye, once returned, refused to go to work: he did not want to lift a finger toward upholding their illegitimate state, Manchukuo, in any direct or indirect way. Instead he remained at home and spent his time—eyes closed, legs folded—in meditation. But underneath the calm, there was rage—rage for the boulders that life had showered down upon his head.

It was Baba, his fourth son, at the boisterous age of eleven—joyful to climb and leap, run and somersault, in the wide-open spaces of Manchuria once more—who bore the brunt of his deep anger.

Yeye struck his forehead. Like a strand of pearls, some thirty doves were again perched in a row across the tile roof, billing, cooing, and defecating, the autumn light glinting off their plumage. Yeye looked at them through cramped, narrowed eyes, for he could not bear the mockery of their return. Why, just that morning, over Number Four Son's tearful protests, he had instructed the help to capture all the birds and transport them deep into the oblivion of the countryside. "Good riddance," he had muttered as he watched the fellow drive off, carting away the birds in their dovecote, the squeaking of the wagon growing fainter and fainter as the mist in the distance engulfed them.

In the afternoon, when Baba came home from school, he whooped and hollered and twirled in giddy circles in the courtyard: yes, his friends had found their way home.

"The birds distract Fourth Son from his studies," Yeye said, but Baba knew this was far from the truth; his father had never taken an interest in educating his children, except for the two oldest boys; each autumn, Baba burned with anxiety as he waited for his father to give him the few yuan for his tuition. He eyed his friends with envy when their parents promptly outfitted them with new school uniforms; and he felt his own shame.

It always comes to this—the day before school, and I must beg for the money. I'd rather be like them: I'd rather be from a poor family with few children. The parents take good care of the one or two they have—unlike us, raised like a mob of barnyard animals, thought Baba.

"Children are *nie zhang*—retribution for the sins of another life. They are a pestilence visited upon a man," Baba had often heard his father say. But why should Yeye have complained so much? He was the eldest son of a rich man; he was never required to work; the Patriarch, Baba's grandfather, provided for everyone under his roof.

Indeed, children could be useful to Yeye on occasion. When he was in the mood for taking a jaunt through the surrounding countryside, swinging his stylish walking stick on a spring morning, Baba was required to follow a few steps behind, toting his father's satchel. A little gentleman-in-waiting. As inconsequential as a seed of sesame. In the afternoon, his ornery parent would indulge in a good meal at a restaurant. "Don't tell your mother about this" were his only words to Baba the entire day.

Children could also be useful after Yeye had had a disagreement with his own father and fallen out of grace. Baba and his brothers and sisters were all herded into the chamber of the Patriarch (the old gentleman, so regal and seemingly out of reach to his grandchildren, may as well have been the Great Jade Emperor up in Heaven), lined up across the room, and made to kowtow in unison, in apology for their parent.

Bong! Bong! Bong! Bong! Their little heads sounded like chestnuts striking the ground in autumn.

"In a large family with several generations living under one roof, children—and I've got seven now!—are nuisance enough without the added pestilence of their pet birds, defecating on top of us all," Yeye grumbled on the afternoon of the doves' return. He shut his eyes and sat cross-legged and tried to meditate; the only noise in the room was the regular sound of his sniffing as he circulated *qi*—the breath of life—through his body. For now, he would focus on exercises in self-cultivation so that he might attain Nirvana at the end of his mortal life. He would forget about the doves that had returned—at least for the moment. He would find some other way to be rid of them. And get rid of them he did.

Baba was heartbroken when his doves were given away to relatives in the countryside, but he comforted himself with the building of another elaborate dovecote from old orange crates.

He knew that within a year's time—by the following fall—he would have raised another flock.

He was familiar with every stage of their growth and development. In spring, two birds that had mated for life produced a pair of eggs, which they took turns incubating; Baba knew that the ungainly, naked young—just pink puffs of flesh—would emerge on the eighteenth day: not a day sooner, not a day later.

He awaited their arrival with terrific eagerness—more enthusiasm than the parent birds appreciated, for on the eighteenth day, over their *hrruu-hrruu* protests, Baba would try to nudge them off their eggs with his hands, to see if there were signs of the emerging squabs. The baby birds that struggled out of the shells were predictably a male and a female. The pair would also come to mate for life.

The parent birds took turns feeding their young until the crops of the squabs were monstrously distended; when they were older, the nestlings nodded and swiveled their heavy heads as they strained with shut eyes to extend their necks. In time, the unlovely young lost their yellow down, and their porcupine quills changed into luminous white plumage. When Baba bounced them on the palms of his hands to feel their weight, they made subdued, reedy sounds. They did not struggle, for he was as familiar to them as their parents.

As soon as their wings were strong enough, Baba trained the fledglings early each morning, before school, to answer his call. They beat their wings furiously and hopped on his fingers in their initial attempts to soar.

"Fly, my little friends, fly away, but always come back to me," said Baba.

In a month's time, they knew Baba's warbling whistle. By the end of the third month, they were strong fliers; when they heard his call, they spiraled and swooped down from high in the open sky to alight upon his head and shoulders; he knew magic to draw them down from the winds.

That summer, Baba paid a visit to his third uncle's family in the countryside; it was an excuse

for a reunion with the birds that had been given away the previous fall. The white doves had mated with wild pigeons, and a new generation of mottled young, each with its own unique markings, fluttered about under the rafters in the barn. The smell of horse manure punctuated the air, and shafts of dusty blue light pierced the chinks in the roof; bird wings flashed silver.

Gazing up at them in the stillness, soft with their cooing, he remembered back to the time when he had held them, placing his face right up against theirs to see the concentric gold rings in their eyes. He remembered the feel of silk as he stroked the long feathers that covered their legs, all the way down to their toes. He thought back on how he had held pearls of dried peas up to their stubby pink beaks. They would not come to him now. They had long forgotten his voice.

With the approach of autumn, Baba's new flock had multiplied and matured. "Whoo-whoo," he cried as he waved his arms each morning and urged the lazy things to fly (the birds preferred to keep the food in their dovecote in sight). Baba ran with them in the wide open fields, watching his flock sweep across the sky in dizzying circles, the sound of their wing beats diminishing as they rose ever higher, becoming tiny white specks that melted into pillows of clouds.

"Please come back!" Baba would silently pray, his heart beating fast; though they had always returned, he could never be sure of it: perhaps a few would join up with someone else's flock. When they reappeared, he silently called the roll. He recognized each one of them, even in flight.

But Baba's increasing pleasure was matched by a growing anxiety: he knew that soon he would be made to give his birds away.

With the arrival of autumn came Little Yao, a sleepy-eyed, thickset cousin with big ears. He hailed from Erlingsuo, which lay in the direction of Inner Mongolia. Yeye recognized an opportunity when he saw one: the birds were foisted off on this cousin. As the young man loaded the dovecote onto the wagon, Baba stood silently by, gazing upon the button eyes of his ruffled, agitated friends. He cried—big, fat salty tears that stung deeply.

"Fly, my little birds, fly away, but please come back to me," he whispered. This time, though, his heart knew it would never be so. Erlingsuo was just too far away.

But as Little Yao climbed onto the sideboard, Baba heard words that he would eternally cherish:

"One must not take away everything that's dear to a child," the voice addressed Yeye. "Leave him this special one." It was the sonorous voice of the Patriarch, with his dense, bristling eyebrows like thick black caterpillars. The old man pointed with his teakwood cane at one particular bird.

"I have seen the boy with this one—this one with the white wings and lavender body . . . just like a butterfly in the sky. I saw it plummet down from way up high to alight softly on the child's shoulders. Yes, yes, you must at least leave him this one. . . ."

IF MY FATHER couldn't have all his doves, he could at least play with the yellow bird that lived with Old Lady and Old Man Lu.

Baba could not remember when the childless couple moved into the mud cottage at the corner of the South Garden. To him, it seemed that they had sprouted from the very soil; they had practical old faces only a garden could grow. Like the ancient well next to their cottage, which provided drinking water for all the families in the neighborhood, the couple were a fixture of the landscape. The Patriarch allowed them to stay on the grounds, provided that they kept an eye on the walled garden.

In the early summer they guarded the ripening ears of corn from the *hui-hui,* untamable men whose ancestors had been nomads in Central Asia; the thieves climbed over the thick earthen wall, which was held intact by the roots of big willows growing along the top.

Chickens and especially ducks, waddling down to the Western Marsh each morning, had to be shooed away from the cabbage, for they not only ate insects and worms; they gobbled up the tender greens as well. Of course, if Old Lady Lu now and then "accidentally" allowed her own flock to escape the confines of her cottage fence, Baba's family "opened one eye, shut the other eye" on the situation.

But the couple's primary duty was to guard the old well to keep the children from falling in; the little ones loved to play near its gaping mouth; on hot days, they cranked up the bucket to douse their nubby heads with a soothing stream; they tossed down stones, brickbats, and roof tiles into its depth, just to hear the *gedong!* when the objects hit water.

Baba liked to toss brickbats too, but most of all, he liked to spend time with the old couple; whenever the idea to visit popped into his head, he would wander ever so slowly into the South Garden, like a cat on a full belly, stopping here and there to sniff wind-borne scents. The old couple never had much to say to him; in fact, they had very little to say to each other: a gesture or half-glance from one, and the other responded seamlessly. (After a lifetime together, not only did their thoughts mirror each other's; so, too, did their features.)

But talk was not what Baba came for; he simply enjoyed watching the old folk go about their activities, which varied according to the rhythm of the seasons. On summer afternoons, the husband did little more than sit in the east end of the cottage, where a feisty little breeze pushed in through the open window. The yellow bird's bamboo cage hung just outside, under the eaves, and the old man would coax a tune out of his feathered companion.

Sometimes, listening to the yellow bird—not one of those flighty finchlike creatures, but a patient, mellow old thing that warbled resolutely upon its perch—Baba would treat himself to a nap upon the old folks' kang and, on waking, sleep-warmed, look about, thinking: When I grow up, I hope I can live in a clean, dry cottage and be left alone to watch over a garden. For

although the House of Yang was wealthy, it was an uncomfortable environment for him: with generations living under the same roof, there was daily discord, arising from gossip, jealousy, and quibbling over large and small matters. And for a child such as Baba, low in the family pecking order, the weight of the elders and Confucian propriety bore down on his little soul like a mountain.

Life was simple for the old couple; they needed very little to live comfortably. They were free to pick cabbage, eggplant, onions and potatoes from the garden. In late spring, when the cattails grew tall along the Western Marsh, the husband went to harvest them. After the cuttings had been left to dry in the sun for a few days, the couple used the stalks to braid big, handsome baskets, which they sold to the fruit vendors. With this money, they were able to buy their rice throughout the summer and early fall.

Another source of income for the husband and wife was Old Lady Lu's queer ability to "jump the spirit": she was a witch doctor, able to minister to the sick. The wealthy and the educated disdained her art and said it was a lot of nonsense, but many of the poor came to seek her help.

One afternoon, as Baba sat on the kang in the cottage, a mother came in with her boy.

Old Lady Lu was seated on a heavy wooden bench, facing the altar that held aloft the image of Great-Grandfather Fox, an old man with thin, slotted eyes and long whiskers—a grim portrait of the spirit manifest in mortal form. The husband burned incense and lit the candles at the altar. His wife closed her eyes.

Dong-dong-dong-dong-chung-chung-chung! The old man struck the fishskin drum and rattled the metal rings at the end of its long handle. Old Lady Lu's body began to quiver and shake: Great-Grandfather Fox had entered her soul.

"The gourd has flowered, the fruit covered with
    hoary hair;
To know the heart of the Immortal, we surely do
    not dare.

Changbai Mountain has caves ancient and deep;
In the shade of pine and cypress the Spirit goes to
    sleep,"

sang Old Man Lu.

When the old woman began flailing her arms and legs, her husband, who stood behind her, pressed her down firmly by the shoulders and chanted:

"The roof is low, the pillars are many;
Too many bumps and scrapes: be wary.
Watch your head and watch your knees;
Too many nicks make us ill at ease."

Her flying arms and legs calmed to a trembling.

"Who wakes me from my dreams?" The old woman's lips moved, but the voice that emerged was not hers. 'Twas that of Great-Grandfather Fox.

"I am the wife of Hu the fishmonger," answered the mother. "I've come to ask the Immortal One to chase away the boy's sickness." She came forward and set her child down upon the old woman's jiggling knees.

With eyes shut tight, and her body bobbing up and down, the old woman felt the lumps and bumps of the boy's skull, meditating upon its topography, and then inserted her chapped brown fingers under his padded jacket to count his tiny ribs. The boy kicked like an overturned tortoise and squealed.

In a quavering baritone, Great-Grandfather Fox deliberated:

"Your boy has tumbled the incense pot in your backyard, the one you placed in honor of the Spirit of the Yellow Weasel. He has also collapsed the opening to the Spirit's den with his nasty stick.

"Within two days, bring me three pairs of red candles, two bundles of incense, a dozen *mantou*—steamed bread rolls—four yards of white cloth, four yards of black cloth, a *jin* of fish, and a *jin* of pork. At that time I will mediate for you with the wrathful Yellow Weasel."

The fishmonger's wife nodded in reverential silence.

The old woman rose to her feet, reached up to the altar, retrieved a brown glass vial, knocked a dab of the powder out onto a square of paper, and folded the medicine into it.

How can she do all this without opening her eyes? Baba wondered.

"Meanwhile, give this to the child at cock's crow," came the voice of Great-Grandfather Fox. Old Lady Lu handed the tiny packet to the mother.

Next, the old woman measured three big spoonfuls of incense ash and folded the powder in yet another square of white paper.

"Dissolve this in boiling water and feed it to him at the same hour. It will quench the fire of his fever."

Baba winced; he knew the taste well; it had made his insides pucker up. Nainai, a country girl with country beliefs, had, against the wishes of Yeye, sought the witch doctor's services to cure Baba's sickness one year. He felt sorry for the child. "He'll be even worse off after drinking that down!" he said to himself.

"Any more requests?" asked Great-Grandfather Fox.

"No," replied the mother, and she bowed to Old Lady Lu, now returned to the bench.

As the *dong-dong-dong-dong-chung-chung-chung* of the fishskin drum sounded with increasing fury, the old woman's shaking grew into a wild thrashing. Her face flushed red. When her husband set aside his drum and grasped her shoulders, her arms and legs stiffened and shot straight out. He held her down for a long while. The room was absolutely silent; even the boy had stopped mewling. Then the old woman's convulsions finally subsided: Great-Grandfather Fox had vacated her soul and had returned to Changbai Mountain, curled up in his cave to dream his dreams.

The old woman opened her eyes. "Ai, where have I been?" she asked in her own voice. "I am very tired and thirsty. Let me lie down for a spell." Her old mate led her to rest on the kang.

When the wild geese flew south in late autumn, there were no more vegetables to be had from the garden. In this season, the deep-green cattails had also withered back into the water

without a murmur; Old Lady Lu and her husband could no longer make baskets. Folk occasionally came to the cottage to see the witch doctor, but the income engendered by "jumping the spirit" was not enough to support them through the winter. It was during the coldest months that Old Lady Lu and her mate strained to hear the whine of trumpets, sounding like a flock of angry geese; where the music came from was where they would be able to fill their bellies.

During La-yue, the month of the twelfth moon (nearing the Spring Festival), big, noisy weddings took place throughout the towns and villages. The celebrations commenced at dawn and lasted well into the night. If the family was wealthy, the celebrations raged three days under a spacious tent, with staggered groups of family and friends arriving at the banquet tables. Waiters bustled in and out of the big kitchen to serve the hundreds of guests.

The hired musicians began their announcement of the wedding day even before sunrise. Baba watched the old couple walk in the direction of the music, each with an iron pail in one hand and, in the other, a cane, to steady his or her steps upon the patches of ice on the ground. When they came to the enormous tent, they found the entrance to the kitchen.

"*Dao xi!* We've come to wish the bride and groom great happiness," the old pair said as they greeted the cooks, the deep furrows of their faces lifted ever so slightly into smiles.

They would not have been turned away on most days; it was unimaginable that they should be turned away on the propitious day of a marriage. The cooks ladled food into their pails from a big ceramic vat that contained leftover soup, vegetables, and meat. It would have been perfectly proper for the couple to join the invited guests at one of the banquet tables, but they had no time to waste: they hurried off with their pails toward the distant clamoring of cymbals, gongs, drums, and trumpets, where yet another wedding was taking place.

On a good day, they collected several pails of food, which they stored in the big ceramic vat in their own kitchen. The food would freeze and could be kept until the spring without spoiling.

Though his father disapproved of eating with beggars, Baba loved nothing better than to join the old couple when they dipped into their meatball-filled vat—a vat big enough for him to hide in.

The food served fresh at the wedding is good, thought Baba. But it's oh so much tastier after it becomes leftovers! The fragrance filled the cottage entirely as the concoction was reheated, and the burbling noises it made caused him to swallow loudly in anticipation. Throughout the winter, the two old people lived quite well on the wedding food.

With the arrival of spring, Baba would, once again, see the familiar figure of Old Man Lu silently harvesting the cattails along the Western Marsh.

Nothing will change . . . they will always be here, my father wished to believe. Just like the old well that's been here forever, providing water, pure and sweet, cool and comforting.

"BE DILIGENT IN your book learning. Be a good person and a dutiful child," my father would often hear the grown-ups admonish. "You don't want to end up like Laifu, do you?" And he saw the younger children wag their heads sideways, for like Baba, they had all been told the story of one well-to-do family in their hometown of Xinmin, a story whose untidy conclusion was enacted in their own days before their very eyes.

It was said that long before Baba was born, a dyeworks was established on East Avenue in Xinmin. Here, for a fee, bolts of plain white cotton cloth brought in by folk were made to blossom with color. The dyeworks also purchased the virgin material that would later be marketed in town and in the neighboring cities as flowing yards of flower prints; the favorite design was snowy garlands on a field of indigo.

The proprietor of the dyeworks was a quiet man named Guo, who wore his silence in a thoughtful manner. Every day he dressed in

work clothes made from coarse blue cloth; even after his business had grown and prospered, he did not think to display his wealth but continued to wear his old clothes. He was known to the people of Xinmin as a generous fellow, but he was most admired for his attentiveness to his wife, who had the timid look of a sparrow.

"Ai, he's so good to her. Rich as he is, he does not take a concubine," people said. "Yes, barren as she is, he remains faithful."

"Not to worry, Old Partner," Guo said to his wife. "Let us go to the Niang-niang Temple and pay our respects to the Goddess of Child-bearing. Surely, she will see the emptiness surrounding our hearth and hearts."

When his wife tired and could not ascend the temple steps on her tiny bound feet, he carried her up pickaback.

At the altar to Niang-niang, they prayed for a filial son, who would carry on the business and comfort them in their old age.

When the prayers at the local temple brought

them no child, the pair made a pilgrimage to faraway Dashiqiao—Big Stone Bridge—to attend the fair at the largest Niang-niang *miao* in Liaoning Province. They arrived on the eighteenth day of the Fourth Month, joined by the thousands of others from near and far, all come to pray for sons and daughters. For hundreds of years, folk had been coming to this particular temple, for Niang-niang was known to be especially attentive here.

According to legend, a farmer from Niuzhuang—Cow Town—on his way to Dashiqiao overtook a woman on the road.

"I cannot walk any farther. Can I ride in your wheelbarrow?" the woman asked him.

As they approached Dashiqiao at dusk, the weight of the woman increased until the farmer could no longer push the vehicle forward. They came to a dead stop at the foot of a mountain.

"Thank you, young man. This is as far as I want to go," the woman said, and she hopped off.

The man watched her figure move swiftly up the steep mountainside, soon to disappear in the blue evening mist. When he related this strange incident to the people of Dashiqiao, they said: "Ah, but you have been honored. There is a small Niang-niang temple at the top of the mountain. It was Niang-niang herself you have brought into our midst!"

The people of Dashiqiao built a bigger, more splendid temple at the foot of the mountain, to honor the arrival of the deity on the eighteenth day of the Fourth Month.

From the guardians of the temple at Dashiqiao, Guo and his wife bought clay figurines known as "mud babies"; they encircled the bellies of the boy mud dolls with scarlet strings, hoping that by so doing, they would soon lasso a real baby of flesh.

That fall, in a year toward the end of the reign of the Guangxu Emperor, a family of refugees from Shandong Province sought shelter at the home of Old Guo and his wife: every two or three years, the ravages of drought, flood, or locusts in the southern provinces drove the hungry to Manchuria. The family was beset with far too many children. The father offered to sell Guo and his wife his youngest, a year-old boy.

The night his family left him, the child crawled to the door and cried and cried, afraid to shut his eyes. But soon he tired and fell asleep on the pillow left for him on the floor.

"Our prayers have been finally answered. We will name him Laifu—Arrival of Prosperity," the new parents said as they looked upon his slumbering, tearstained face. "He has a wide forehead, which can only mean that he is of high intelligence."

With the passage of the months, the boy's heart slowly relinquished the memories of his birth parents and came to know only Guo and his wife.

When Laifu was five, a tutor was found to teach him the Four Books and the Five Classics—thoughts of Confucius that guided men to piety and moral conduct. He was also taught arithmetic.

Laifu was a precocious child; by age fifteen, he was skillful enough on the abacus to help keep the books for his father's business. By age twenty, he was traveling to the neighboring cities and towns—Shenyang, Yingkou, Zhangwu, Faku—distributing bolts of flower prints to the dry goods stores and collecting money owed to the dyeworks.

Folk respectfully addressed him as Shao-dongjia—Young Master—for he had grown into a handsome, self-assured man. His somber eyes were big and unfathomably dark, which instilled not a little fear in even his old parents. Laifu spent money freely and carried himself with the swagger appropriate to a "young master."

"Young Guo is good to deal with," people commented. "He calls one one, two two—a man of his word. Never tries to shortchange us." The shopkeepers and innkeepers courted him, entertaining him at theaters and restaurants. Away from his family, young Laifu learned to drink, to womanize, to gamble, but worst of all, he learned to smoke opium, a drug that hoisted his spirits and sustained him at the gaming table through the night.

Old Guo worried about the changes he saw in his son. "We must find him a good woman to keep an eye on him," he said to his wife. "Marriage will cure him of the many evil habits he has learned on the road."

They found him a girl from a respectable family in Xinmin, but no amount of watching by a sharp-eyed wife did him any good. Not only did he continue to gamble and smoke opium; he also involved himself more deeply in the activities of the secret societies run by hooligans in town. He spent most of his time at their gaming table, playing *paijiu*—dominoes—wrapped in a haze of opium smoke. The gamblers loved his company, for not only was he generous, lavishing money on his friends, but when he lost, he always paid up without the least bit of prodding.

There was a saying among the people: "As soon as a man enters a gambling den, the foundation of his home begins to tremble and quake. The few seconds that it takes for him to lose at the table are the seconds it takes for his house to come down on his head."

As time went on, Laifu did not bother to try to hide his transgressions from his old parents; he helped himself to larger sums from the dyeworks to feed his habits.

Old Guo, who had weathered over sixty winters, could not weather the betrayal of his son. He fell ill and lay in bed, muttering unintelligibly, his long, gaunt figure fevered under the quilt.

"The old man died from anger," the folk in Xinmin said when Old Guo's life floated away.

A large plot was acquired for a family cemetery. Willow saplings were planted on the grounds.

Now that his father was gone, Laifu was no longer the Young Master but Da Laoban—the Big Boss. He was free to spend money as he wished; there would be no one to reprimand him.

Old Woman Guo, hobbling on her bound feet, knew little about the finances of the dyeworks; as with the women of her time, she did not involve herself in business. She only realized their ruin the day the dyeworks was shut down, the property sold to pay Laifu's debts. She died soon after, wearing her timidness to the grave.

When Laifu had also gambled away the roof over their heads, his wife returned to her mother's home; he himself moved into a tiny room at a boardinghouse. He continued to gamble, wagering small amounts from the sale of his belongings. He could no longer afford opium, but he could still purchase morphine, whose effect was quicker: it was shot directly into the bloodstream.

Within two years of his mother's death, he had sold just about everything. The gamblers were no longer happy to see him; folk eyed him suspiciously, for they feared that a penniless addict would turn to stealing.

But Laifu did not sink to theft. Despite his tattered dress, he continued to comport himself with his back straight and his head held high. He stopped visiting friends, for fear of frightening them unnecessarily.

Day or night, as he walked past the gates of friends and neighbors, or when he approached someone—anyone—on the street, he would put the back of his hand to his ashen face and cough once or twice to announce that he, Laifu, was among them; it was a declaration to the world that he did not sneak around, stepping softly to snatch what did not belong to him.

Now, this is the point at which Laifu's story becomes part of my father's ballooning perception of the world. Baba in his thirteenth year would often see Laifu in all his straight-boned shabbiness pass by the gate at the House of Yang and hear him cough his prideful cough.

Not surprisingly, as time went on and Laifu continued in his impoverished but independent way, Baba heard people remark that the man had integrity. "Ai, it's just too bad he gambles and smokes opium. But one must admit, he does not lack for a bit of backbone: he does not steal, does not beg, does not cling to old relationships. He owes no one."

When everything had been sold—down to

the last pair of his mother's tiny embroidered shoes—Laifu went to the cemetery one midsummer night. It was a night for friends to play chess in the garden; a night for neighbors to gossip, fanning themselves under the stars; a night swelling with promise. After kowtowing at his parents' graves—two adjacent conical mounds of dirt—he carefully placed his tatty old shoes with the tips pointing toward the headstones, as if to say, "I'm sorry. I now come to honor you as a filial son should." Then he padded in his bare feet across the ground, damp with dew, to a weeping willow, with its curtain of trailing branches; fireflies lighted his path. The trees had matured in the years since the death of his father. In the morning, the villagers found him dangling from a noose, his body swaying like foliage.

"Old Guo and his wife must have cheated Laifu in the previous life. The fellow came after them disguised as their own precious child to even the score," Baba heard the townsfolk say in the ensuing days, trying to make sense of the events. "Ai, when Laifu spent Old Guo's last copper, he had fully avenged himself. He knew it was time to go. Always remember, *'Yin guo bao ying'*—'We reap what we sow'—if not in this life, to be sure in the next."

To the grown-ups' didactic "Be a filial, loyal child—you don't want to end up like Guo Laifu, do you?" Baba could not chirp a "no" along with the younger children. In my father's dilating view of the people all about him, he could no longer pronounce simple judgments upon each of their ways.

No, he did not want to come to a sad end like Laifu, as parents suggested that a bad child undoubtedly would, but he knew with certainty that even when he would no longer be able to recall Laifu's face he would, with respect, remember the man's cough, arising not from his throat but from somewhere deep within his soul.

THE YEAR THAT Guo Laifu, who grew up a pampered child wearing embroidered "tiger shoes," met his self-inflicted end, my father was introduced to one who in his childhood wore only pig dung between his bare toes and was still struggling to raise himself above the muck of poverty.

In that summer, when a boil in the back of Baba's right ear grew throbbingly big, Nainai, my grandmother, said to him: "You can go see Daye—Big Uncle—who's recently opened up a practice in town."

"But, Mother, everyone calls this new doctor a quack," Baba protested.

"Don't listen to the gossip," Nainai replied. "My eyes do not deceive me: that fellow has the sure hands of a healer."

And so Baba paid a visit to Daye's dark little office, which smelled of herbs, fungus, and dust. There, the doctor brought out seven long silver acupuncture needles and worked the cold points into the base of Baba's neck. He also ground

dried medicinal plants into powder and fed the bitter concoction to his doubtful young patient.

By the following morning, the fevered pain had subsided. In two weeks, the boil had disappeared altogether. There was no need to subject Baba to the knife.

With the astonishingly quick cure, Baba grew eager for the tale of Daye's life, which he later heard the Patriarch, his grandfather, recount in detail.

Here was another personality, a mystery in its singularity, another life in my father's unfolding life.

Daye was a poor relation. When he was just a boy, his father gambled away the family home, land, and animals in the ancestral village of Shantuozi and died shortly after. He left Daye to fend for himself. The boy managed to fill his rice bowl by hiring himself out as a pigherd. When it came time for him to marry, he could find no one willing to wed a homeless young man who smelled of swill. In his search for a wife, he sought the assistance of his uncle, the Patriarch of the House of Yang in Xinmin City.

The Patriarch threw the weight of his reputation and wealth behind his nephew. A tiny snip of a peasant girl was finally found who would consent to marry the young man.

The newlyweds moved from the countryside to Xinmin and rented a room on Back Street, just behind the House of Yang.

The wife was good at flipping wheat flour pancakes on the griddle. Daye hawked them in a big willow basket he carried upon his back. He was a familiar figure on the streets: long limbs, long stride, and a long stretch of a face. "*Dabingzi!* Come get your fresh *dabingzi!*" he cried. The couple lived frugally, themselves eating only pancakes made from the less costly cornmeal.

Daye and his wife muddled out a living in this manner for many years.

"Nephew, you cannot continue this hardscrabble existence," the Patriarch said to him one day. "Let me send you to your cousin, my number three son in the city of Zhengjiatun, on the border of Inner Mongolia. He's now the branch manager of the Central Bank of Manchukuo. I am certain he will be able to arrange some other sort of business for you, which will be more profitable."

In Zhengjiatun, the cousin rented a dozen mud cottages and set the husband and wife up as innkeepers. The wife cooked and cleaned for the travelers. Daye fixed the roofs, plastered the walls, and looked after the travelers' horses.

Their new enterprise was no moneymaker either, but they fared somewhat better than in their days as peddlers of pancakes.

Not long after they had settled into their new way of life, an old traveling doctor came to stay at the inn.

During the day, the man wandered the streets of Zhengjiatun, jangling the healer's trademark ring-shaped rattle, thus announcing his arrival to those whose bodies were in need of some mending and repairing.

The doctor was alone in the world. Daye and his wife, like most countryfolk, were generous souls; they looked after the solitary old man even after he had fallen ill and could no longer pay for room and board.

"You've been like a son and daughter to me," said the old man to Daye and his wife. "I'd like to repay your kindness. If you're willing, I'll pass on to you family secrets in the art of healing. In my sole possession are invincible recipes for the repair of broken bones and joints, for that, as you know, is my specialty. With the recipes, you'll never find yourselves abegging. Guard the secrets jealously, for it'll be your ever-replenishing rice bowl."

This was a godsend. Daye felt highly honored: family recipes were passed down for generations from fathers to sons. (By custom, they were not handed down to daughters, for girls would eventually belong to their husbands' clans.)

The doctor began rigorously to train his diligent pupil, teaching him how to handle the tools of the trade. Daye had an aptitude for the healing arts, and because he had been schooled in the Five Classics and the Four Books, the core of Confucian education, the memorizing of prescriptions came easily to him. In a short period of time, the potent recipes were etched in his memory.

Soon after Daye had begun his own practice, the old doctor passed away. The couple buried him in a respectable casket and erected a headstone to honor him as they would have honored their own fathers.

On the streets of Zhengjiatun, *ga-lang, ga-lang* went the rattle that Daye had inherited from the old doctor.

But business was not so good. What first began as whispers soon became loud talk: "That simpleton's got the nerve to call himself a doctor. The fellow's just an innkeeper. The only thing he's qualified to patch up are the holes in the roof."

As the saying goes: "Good news does not leave one's front door, but bad news travels ten thousand li." Soon townsfolk were stabbing their fingers at Daye on the streets and calling him horse doctor, quack, impostor.

"Old partner," Daye said to his wife, his long face stretched even longer in sadness. "This place has never been home. Let us return to Xinmin and start anew. There we'll have the comfort of being closer to my uncle."

So one summer, man and wife closed down the inn, packed up their belongings, and returned to Back Street, where they set up shop, hanging above the door a sign that read: "Doctor Yang. Will minister to all ailments. Specialist in injuries to bones and joints. Secret family recipes."

Well, it wasn't exactly false advertisement: Daye possessed secret family recipes, rightly enough; they just weren't *his* family's recipes.

This was the summer that Baba made his fortunate acquaintance with Daye and his seven long acupuncture needles and was so speedily cured.

Though the House of Yang, his own kinsmen, had only high praise for his skills, other folk in Xinmin were not so impressed by the new healer in town. "I recognize this Doctor Yang," Baba heard the neighbors say. "Yes, I remember that long nose on that face shaped like a shoehorn. I don't recall any men of medicine in the Yang Clan. What secret family recipes? Probably just recipes for those pancakes he used to peddle. I can still smell the grease and onions on him."

And just as in Zhengjiatun, the people called Daye a quack and a charlatan. Business was bad.

"I guess it was not so smart for us to come back to Xinmin—not the place for my upstart practice, at any rate. Old partner, we must make another move. It seems we are forced to go among strangers once again." And as always, without a chirrup of complaint, the wife packed up their things and followed her husband to a new place. They settled in a remote town to the northwest of Xinmin, where doctors were few. There they hung up their sign.

This time, Daye had made the right move. No one knew his past. Business was quite good.

He earned a comfortable living and gained a reputation as a man of good medicine; no one called him names.

In the year following his relocation, a man of great wealth from the big city of Shenyang, to the northeast of Xinmin, was heard to be searching far and wide for a doctor to heal a stubborn leg wound. Traveling in the country-side, his party had been ambushed by "red-beards," bandits, and the magnate was shot in the leg. The bullet was removed, but the wound refused to close and the broken bone would not mend. His condition worsened with the passing weeks. Illustrious doctors of Western medicine were consulted, but each one informed the man that his leg had to be amputated.

Needless to say, he was not happy with their diagnoses. He searched the neighboring cities—Liaozhong, Xinmin, Liaoyang, Zhangwu, and even Daye's remote township—for a healer who possessed the power to save his leg. He invited doctors of both traditional and Western medi-cine to a meeting in Shenyang. Daye was re-quested to attend and was graciously escorted to the city.

But the general consensus of those at the conference was that the man's leg could not be saved. If the leg was amputated, his life would be assured; if the leg should remain and the wound continued to fester, he would most cer-tainly lose his life. No doctor wanted to forgo amputation and later be punished for mal-practice.

"I can save your leg, Your Honor," Daye said to the great man of power and wealth as he stood alone among the gathering of the wise. "I'm willing to stake my insignificant life upon the success of my cure."

What began as a low thrumming in the great hall became a wave of silent condemnation. Many shook their heads. A country bumpkin knows no better than to throw his own life away, they all said.

The magnate stared long and hard at this tall, unblinking rustic and then silently nodded his consent.

Sure enough, within a week, under Daye's care, the wound began to heal. A half year later, the break in the bone had mended—the man was walking without a limp. Heaven had smiled on the doctor.

"He is a god! I'll have him installed as head of the department of herbal medicine at the medical institute of this city," the man proclaimed. And true to his words, he elevated Daye to this exalted position.

The newspapers wrote marvelous accounts of Daye's medical skills and healing powers. In the ensuing years, Daye's fame and fortune continued to spiral upward, yet there was one wish of his that had gone unfulfilled: he hoped to pass on the healing arts to his son. But the young man—in the same mold as his father: long limbs, long stride, and a long stretch of a face—had other plans and refused to follow in his father's footsteps.

Daye being rather a progressive thinker (and having no other choice), his hope came to rest upon his other child—a daughter. Now, this daughter—a short, squat, swarthy woman with bulbous eyes and yellow, ratlike teeth that sprouted between her normal adult ones, leaning every which way like disrupted roof tiles—was so homely, she aroused pity and brought silent condolences to people's lips.

Daye's daughter, realizing she had little prospect of acquiring a husband, knew she had to acquire some means of self-support. This spurred her to apprentice under her father.

Years later, Baba, at the House of Yang, heard through the grapevine that after completing her studies, the daughter returned to the remote town to the northwest of Xinmin where her father's practice had first flourished and where doctors were still few.

My father heard it rumored that she had hung up her own sign: "Doctor Yang. Will minister to all ailments. Specialist in injuries to bones and joints. Secret family recipes."

This time, it was no false advertisement.

A DAB OF CLOUD scuttled across the unblemished sky like a white mouse.

"What do you think? A rain cloud? You think it might rain?" Baba heard folk ask one another as they rubbed their chins and scratched their heads. They searched their neighbors' faces for a confirmation of the hope.

In Baba's thirteenth summer, the sorghum reached only the height of a man's shoulders and withered.

Sorghum was the staple of the North. Now all that was left to eat was a heavy, coarse meal—a mixture of corn and soybean.

As a precautionary measure, children were not allowed more than a bowl and a half of the stuff, for it ballooned inside the stomach after fluids were taken; and since folk were likely to drink a lot of water after eating the salty, fermented bean sauce that was the ubiquitous accompaniment to northern meals, gluttony was especially dangerous; it was rumored that some had burst their stomachs and died in great agony.

The following spring, the sky again promised to be tightfisted: it was the second year into the drought.

"Last year, the Almanac said there were to be nine dragons spouting water. Should have been a decent year for rain, but there was hardly a drop," said Nainai, my grandmother, with a sniff of disgust.

She consulted the Imperial Almanac. Each yearly issue gave a forecast of the amount of rain that would fall upon the land and offered other vital information, such as favorable days for births and marriages, appropriate days for funerals, safe days for journeys, lucky days for raising roof beams and moving furniture. The Almanac was all that one needed to negotiate the uncertainties of life.

"This year, it says there are to be twelve dragons in the sky. Aiya, really terrible . . . twelve lazy dragons!" said Nainai.

"But, Mother, doesn't more dragons mean more rain?" asked Baba.

"No, of course not. Remember the adage about the monks?"

Baba shook his head.

" 'One thirsty monk will use a shoulder pole to carry two buckets of water; two thirsty monks will shoulder only one bucket of water on a pole between them; three thirsty monks will remain three thirsty monks.'

"This is also the way of the dragons: the more dragons there are for rainmaking, the more each will shuck his share of the work."

April brought no rain. May brought no rain. The men and women of Xinmin looked up at the azure sky through eyes slotted by doubt and fear. The sun buckled the earth, shaking dust into the air.

"If there's no rain this year, we won't even have the early-season crops of soybean and corn. Everyone's sick of the stuff—just the smell of it makes me ill—but it is better than the thin, dry odor of hunger," the people said. Their stomachs anticipated the grinding of emptiness; hunger was an inherited remembrance.

"We must pray to Dragon King for rain," the elders advised. "We have neglected him for too long." Ancient prayers were dusted off in their memories.

Dragon King, the severe but reasonable ruler of the oceans and rivers, the great creator of the Yellow River—the cradle of Chinese civilization. Dragon King, the source of life.

On a June morning, a day decreed by the mayor of Xinmin, business owners and residents along the main thoroughfares burned incense upon outdoor tables set up to honor the god. Flowing calligraphy on vermilion paper posted upon the walls above the tables read: "Dragon King, the rainmaker, the ruler of the five lakes, four oceans, nine rivers, and eight streams, is enthroned among us."

On this appointed day, each family was required to send one male representative to the site of the largest well in the city, there to join the multitude in paying homage to the heavenly rainmaker. Baba eagerly volunteered to represent the House of Yang; permission was quickly granted, as no one else had a midge of desire for the job.

Baba arrived at the site clad only in shorts; upon his head rested a crown of braided willow; the tender green shoots feathering down to his shoulders provided scant protection from the sun. Similarly outfitted were all the men and boys who sought audience with Dragon King.

A table set against the well displayed candles and incense, and these were lit as the mayor read a prayer to Dragon King that had been written in vermilion ink upon a sheet of yellow paper:

"We have come before you, O Dragon King, to make an entreaty to your generous soul: O bringer of life, grace our land with rain, for without water to our fields, we will have nothing for the winter stores.

"If you should grant us rain this summer, O Lord, we the folk of Xinmin will dedicate ourselves to raising a glorious new temple in your honor."

Baba thought: It's just like what Mama says to bribe my little sister when she's a nuisance: "If you are a good girl, come New Year, Mother will make you a pretty little jacket to wear."

A modest temple to Dragon King was already in existence on the outskirts of Xinmin, along the bank of the river Liu. It had been forgotten during the years of good rains; the fiery red of the temple pillars had long been extinguished and had turned a powdery pink, but no one thought to repaint them. No one came to make offerings; the local incense business trickled down to nothing. Now that the people needed help from Dragon King, they could not do enough to accommodate him. The incense business picked up considerably.

After the prayer, the mayor burned the yellow paper and kowtowed at the mouth of the well. The gathering, following his movements, bowed in silence.

As the kneeling men and boys covered the ground like thousands of ripened melons in a patch, fifteen monstrous red drums, each carried by two men, and fifteen sets of cymbals entered the scene, to boom and crash a reminder to Dragon King: "Lest you've forgotten, O Great One, this is what the sound of rainmaking is like."

Water from the well, flung from buckets, doused the grateful men and boys. Another reminder: "Lest you forget, O Dragon King, this is what rain looks like."

Afterward, following the lead of the mayor and other dignitaries, the crowd wended its way across town, itself looking like the long, thrashing tail of a dragon.

The persistent *doong-doong-doong-doong!* of the drums troubled the earth; the heavy pulse invaded Baba's soul through the bottoms of his bare, marching feet. The cymbals clamored like ten thousand angry wives flinging washbasins, the vibrations rattling the desiccated leaves upon treetops and clattering the bowls in the cupboards.

The Japanese vice mayor, among the handful of Japanese officials in attendance, was the most devout of the supplicants, displaying an unparalleled zeal. (The Japanese had been in Manchuria for nearly a decade but, on the whole, were unobtrusive; they held subordinate titles such as Vice Mayor, Assistant Superintendent

of Schools, or Deputy Chief of Police, but de facto power was in their hands. Most folk had little or no direct dealings with them. Schoolchildren, however, were given their daily doses of Japanese-language lessons by stern Japanese teachers.) The vice mayor, overpowered by primal music, danced and weaved like a drunkard through the streets.

Women along the parade route readied tubs of water to shower upon the procession.

By the end of the afternoon, all the larger wells in Xinmin had been visited with prayers. The people dispersed. Baba returned home, limp, dusty, and cooked as pink as shrimp.

Sure enough, three days after the ceremony, the sky came to boil with black clouds. Lightning! and then *gooloong, gooloong, goolooloo-loong!* sounded high above. The dragons were at work, threading through the thunderheads that had conspired farther north.

The rain came down. Not tickling rain, as fine as the hair on the nape of a cow: that kind foretold only more of the same. No, it was a steady downpour, which fingered through the soil, deeply massaging the earth. Ah, the smell of rain! Dragon King had heard their entreaties.

Baba watched the sorghum grow to its full height that season; the tassels of the ripened grain turned russet—a red to warm men's hearts.

The people of Xinmin kept their promise: by fall, work had begun on the new temple, upon the site of the old.

Throughout the numbing winter, carpenters labored to carve symbols of good omen upon the beams and latticework; craftsmen molded statues of gods and spirits from clay; artists breathed upon their brushes to keep the pigments from freezing upon the hairs as they painted murals.

On an April day, Baba joined the hordes at the opening ceremony. Vendors hawked live ducks and geese, pinwheels made from bamboo, and candied haws, which children clamored for. A temporary stage was erected, upon which opera singers contributed their share to the general cacophony.

Baba was eager to meet Dragon King. He squeezed into the temple, which smelled wonderfully of fresh paint and lacquer. In the temple hall he was hailed by a figure with the head of a dragon—a furry mustache under a bulbous red nose, protruding eyes, sharp teeth, and antlers—and the body of a human being, who, standing arms akimbo, wore the long yellow robe of an emperor. When he could get close enough, Baba ran his fingers over the carved folds of the robe.

To either side of the god were his lieutenants: unsavory-looking characters with heads of fish, turtle, crab, and prawn. Behind them spread the deep green bottom of the sea, brimming with creatures that swam between the columns of the god's shimmering crystal palace. Baba's head was made dizzy by the splendor of the artists' imaginings.

The ensuing summer was also a season of plentiful rain; the tassels on the sorghum had grown a foot long. But just before the harvest, suddenly, the rivers Liu and Liao, converging just south of Xinmin, swelled and overflowed their banks. Rainfall had been normal in Xinmin, but there had been torrential rains to the northwest, in the direction of Inner Mongolia. The water surged over the banks and drowned the fields, leaving only the tassels of the sorghum to thrash about above the bull-roaring, murky water.

"How did we come to deserve this?" the people asked. "We've broken our backs to build a temple in honor of Dragon King, yet the water still works against us."

Seers (the only beneficiaries of crises and tears) were consulted.

One said: "You have forgotten about the very powerful Catfish Demon. His magic has grown to fearsome proportions, for he has spent the last two thousand years in meditation. You have aroused his jealousy by all the fuss over Dragon King and his attendant spirits. Now this demon of the rivers is throwing a tantrum. A temple must be built in his honor if you want to soothe and smooth down the waters."

Baba attended the noisy grand opening of the temple to the Catfish Demon and gazed in awe upon the exquisite ugliness of the god's liver-colored, bewhiskered face.

In the following year, the rivers were well behaved and the sky accommodating. And as before, the incense business went into a decline.

"How come we're going to Badaohaodao so late at night?" Baba asked his cousin as they joined the trail of folk from Shantuozi on their yearly Ghost Festival pilgrimage.

It was summer vacation, and my father had journeyed from his hometown of Xinmin to Shantuozi, the ancestral village of the Yang Clan, where the Great Progenitor had first settled upon the Manchurian plains.

"Shhh! Just come along. I'll tell you a story when we get back," the cousin replied, with a look of keen solemnity.

Lanterns bobbed, glowing like a multitude of fireflies.

At the junction of the small village road and Badaohaodao—the Road of Eight Trenches—men and women lit incense and kowtowed. They burned "spirit money"—money for the dead—yellow paper cut in the shape of coins: the souls of the departed would need currency in the afterlife to bribe their way out of punishments in Hell or to speed their journey to Heaven.

After the ceremony, they returned home, and Baba sat in the darkness of the back garden, listening to his cousin tell of two luckless souls who had met upon Badaohaodao road in the darkness very long ago.

The wind blowing from the direction of the river raked the leaves of the pear trees. "Field chickens"—frogs—burped in unison deep within the well, but these sounds were lost to Baba as his cousin's tale bore him back into the years.

In the first decade of the century, an orphan no more than twelve years old arrived in Shantuozi—Hamlet of the Shan Clan—looking for work. Where he came from, no one knew.

"Your skin is so black, your blood must run black too," the village boys would say to him.

"No, it is red like yours," he would reply. "Here, I'll show you," and he made a small cut on the back of his forearm with a sickle, like a fruit vendor attesting to the ripeness of a watermelon. Ruby beads squeezed out of the wound.

The children chimed in agreement: "Yah, you're right. Your blood really is red."

Folk took an immediate liking to the swarthy young fellow; no cloud of deceit ever skimmed across his smooth, round face. When he played with the cowherds in the pasture, his laughter boomed above all the others'.

He was strong for his age, so the villagers hired him on to do grown men's work; but only a child's wage did they pay him. In spite of this injustice, he worked earnestly—it seemed, with all his heart—for the orphan intended Shantuozi to be his home.

Because he was as sturdy and tough as a *gar*, the wooden toy in the shape of a big olive pit that children sent hurtling through the air with a bat, folk called him Dong Gar. In time, no one could recall what his given name really was.

In unsettled times, mounted bandits known as *honghuzi*—the redbeards—flourished; they scourged the countryside like locusts. Farmers in the fields tilled the land with guns slung across their backs to keep the outlaws from taking their draft animals. The redbeards attacked the villages and relieved the countryfolk of their few valuables. In the poorer hamlets they did not steal but, instead, demanded to be fed. Folk were forced to slaughter their precious pigs and host the redbeards for days. When their bellies were full, the unruly guests rode off to harvest the fattened pigs in the next hamlet over.

Upon Old Granddaddy Hill, in the heart of Shantuozi, lookouts were posted to watch for the appearance of redbeards on the horizon. *Gong! Gong! Gong!* The alarm was sounded when they were seen to surface on the edge of the land like flies alighting on the windowsill. (The alarm simultaneously signaled the direction of attack.)

Gua! Gua! Gua! Hundreds of startled crows took to the sky, flying out from the cypresses that crowned the hill and curdling the very air.

Villagers fired at the marauders. If the redbeards dismounted to walk beside their horses, it was to signal that they were only passing through—on their way to bully some other unfortunate village. If the redbeards remained upon their swift steeds, the villagers feared for their chickens, feared for their pigs—feared for their very lives.

Shantuozi was ringed by a tall wall of spiked willow posts. Farmers herded their cattle back in through the gates when they heard the alarm sound; the gateway closed after them. Marksmen entered the trenches at the foot of the wall, to shoot through the chinks between the posts.

Dong Gar was strong. Dong Gar was courageous. Dong Gar was a crack shot to boot. Whenever the alarm sounded, he was tossed a rifle by one of the wealthier villagers, who could afford firearms.

One fell day, redbeards broke through the gates and folk ran trembling to hide in their homes. But Dong Gar stood his ground, his grim eyes flashing white. He calmly drew his gun to his shoulder as the rabble leader rode toward him.

"One last bullet," he said. "I have saved one last bullet. My skill has never failed me."

Piang! The bullet hit the pommel of the lead- er's saddle, just where Dong Gar had aimed. The head redbeard turned tail and fled, taking his men out the gate with him like a string of beads.

During winter, on the day of a wedding, Dong Gar, given a gun and a horse, was asked to guard the bride and her relatives, riding in a treasure-laden wagon to the house of the groom.

On one occasion, as a wedding party attempted to cross the frozen river Liu, four bandits from neighboring Heishanxian—Black Mountain Village—advanced on them.

"Stay low, driver!" Dong Gar ordered, the fire of wrath burning upon his black brow. "On my signal, speed the wagon across!

"The rest of you get down! Lie flat on the ice!

"Yah, driver! Let's go!"

As the redbeards closed in, Dong Gar used the wagon as a shield, wheeling away to the front, to the side, as he dodged the bullets. Skilled at shooting from a running horse, he answered their shots. Two redbeards were hit; they tumbled off their horses and did not rise again. One was wounded and captured. The fourth man rode away.

Dong Gar could count on his own strength, courage, and skill, but he certainly could not count on his luck, which abandoned him as he battled yet another band of redbeards that same winter: perhaps bandits from Heishanxian, come to revenge their fallen comrades. He was just twenty-one when a bullet pierced his heart.

The people of Shantuozi buried him outside the village, along a desolate stretch of the Badaohaodao road. His was an unmarked grave among the other unmarked graves of the homeless—men without families to honor their memories. With the passage of the years, the wind from the northwest, blowing in yellow sand from Mongolia, ate away the conical mound that was his grave.

Folk were in the habit of grazing their cattle along Badaohaodao, but after the death of Dong Gar, they avoided the area—avoided travel on the road. Strange things began to occur: cattle stampeded; horses spooked and galloped off with their wagons in tow, taking the poor wagoners hostage. People said the animals could see what men could not: they were witnesses to ghosts.

The year Dong Gar died, Carpenter Wang of Shantuozi was in his fifties—an age, as the saying goes, when a man should be wise enough to know himself.

"When I was your age, why, I was so strong, I could lift one end of a roof beam by myself while four, five men supported the other end. That's how strong I was," said the old man to his fellow carpenters. He rested his tools, picked up his long pipe, and planted the stem in his mouth, signaling that he was prepared to talk at length.

"Granddad, you must also be very brave, for strength is wasted on cowards," said one young man, slipping a sly smile to the others.

"Heh heh heh," the carpenter laughed. His face wrinkled into a smile of self-satisfaction. "Yes, you can say that. I've been known to wrestle down demons." He sent smoke rings sailing over his head.

"One year, at the big opening of a new temple, when all the folk were watching the abbot light the candles at the altar, a crooked old woman slithered up the temple wall as quick as a lizard. Way up there on top of the roof, she hopped around and cursed up a storm. While everyone just stared, eyes poppin' out with fear, I went up after the old gal, clamped her under one arm, and fetched her back down.

" 'Aiiiee! I am the spirit of the rat,' she screeched, and flopped on the ground like a fish on dry land. 'Your temple is stoppin' up the opening to my hole. I'll put a jinx on all of you!'

"Well, I knew just what to do. I got out a big ol' needle from my toolbox, stabbed the end of her nose with it, and read an incantation over her. In less time than it takes to smoke a bowl of tobacco, she quit her wigglin' and fussin'; I chucked that rat demon right out of her body."

Whether his audience believed his prowess or not, they nodded and looked appropriately spellbound.

Because he was getting on in years, time settling upon his shoulders like lead, Carpenter Wang no longer did heavy work; instead he built furniture and carved the fine details in the latticework over windows and doors.

He owned a set of eighteen woodcarving knives, which he was inordinately proud of. Whenever anyone asked about them, he went on at length:

"These here are my trusty swords. Never let 'em out of my sight. Forged especially for me by a master in the big city of Fengtian. There ain't a soul on this wide earth who can match the man's work." The carpenter had fashioned a special box to cradle his tools.

One winter, in the month of November, he was asked to build a set of bridal cabinets for a family in Shaojiadi—Land of the Shao Family. The eldest son was to bring home a wife before the Spring Festival.

An uninhabited stretch of twenty li lay between Shantuozi and Shaojiadi. A patch here and a patch there were cultivated, but most of it lay unclaimed except by grasses and solemn old willows. Up before dawn, the carpenter walked the great distance to work; if a rare wagon was available, he hitched a ride. He insisted on returning home each evening, for with age, he had become set in his ways and could not imagine sleeping anywhere but upon his own warm kang.

On the day that the cabinets were completed, the master of the house said:

"The sun's low on the horizon, Lao Wang. It's too late for you to be walking home. It's rumored that Badaohaodao is a playground for demons and ghosts. Why not spend the night here?"

"Don't worry about me. I've never been one to be bothered by ghosts," replied the carpenter, with a loud thump to his chest. "I know powerful incantations to throw them off my track."

"The road will be long and the night cold. You must at least have supper with us and empty a bottle of *baigar* to fend off the chill," said the master of the house.

After tossing down his sixth cup of fiery sorghum whiskey to cap off the meal, the carpenter set his fox fur hat firmly upon his head, slung his toolbox upon his ax handle, set the ax upon his shoulder, and headed for home.

It was a moonless night, but the snow on the ground emitted its own subdued light, allowing the old man to see his way.

Gazhi, gazhi—the snow complained under his feet as he lurched happily on, his spirit buoyed by the *baigar*.

Now, he had not gone very far along Badaohaodao when he heard behind him an urgent whisper:

"Carpenter Wang."

"Aiya, that's surely my name," he mumbled, and turned around. There was no one. Only the empty gray road spilling back toward Shaojiadi and the motionless, gnarled, watching willows on either side.

"Indeed, the whiskey must be playing tricks on me. Must have been an owl hooting. Owls . . . owls are bad omens," he muttered, and walked on.

"Carpenter Wang! Carpenter Wang!" There could be no mistake. It was he who was being summoned. Again he spun around; but just as before, there was no one. A chill of fear crept over his heart; he pulled his neck down into the collar of his padded jacket, like a turtle retracting into its shell.

All these years, he had been boasting about his skill in fighting demons and ghosts; he prayed that the good magic would not desert him now.

He removed his hat and, with the palm of his right hand, briskly brushed back his head of stiff, bristly hair. This motion allowed the *yangqi,* positive human energy, to flow forth, suppressing the *yinqi,* the negative energy possessed by demons.

"Spirits can move only along the wheel ruts; I've got to get out of them and walk in the center of the road, where horses go," he said.

The fire of the *baigar* was beginning to subside; he was now shivering. With his collar pulled way up, his own uneven breathing echoed in his ears, sounding like the breathing of some-one rushing at him. He felt, rather than saw, black forms rear from the darkness that encircled him. He broke into a trot.

"Why didn't dear old Ma and Pa give me an extra pair of legs? I've got to get along faster," he said to himself, mopping beads of cold sweat from his brow.

"Ah, this is no good . . . the darkest section of Badaohaodao . . . I need stronger magic to protect me." As he stumbled on, he recited the Incantation of the Five Thunder, followed by the Incantation of Zhongkui the Demon Chaser, all the while pressing his thumb against his fingers in a magic sequence.

Whoop! Something behind him sent his hat flying off his head. He careened forward and scooped it up from the snow.

"After him! Bind him! Tie him up!" he heard hard by. Terror overcame him like a blade of ice stabbed through his heart; his short legs were carrying him forward as fast as they could possibly go.

"Thrash him! Beat him up!"

And suddenly—*gatagatagagata!* The toolbox began to rattle and shake as if possessed. The faster he ran, the more furiously it rattled. One by one, his eighteen "trusty swords" leaped out of the box and hurtled into the night.

Whoop! His hat was sent flying from his head once again, but this time he did not even think to pick it up. He ran on blindly, savagely, breathing so hard his lungs became like the crusty bark of an old pine. And as he thrashed about, flailing his arms like a bewildered bird, he lost his toolbox and his ax. He did not know that he had already lost his shoes and socks; his feet were bleeding, but he could no longer feel the pain.

By the time he reached his garden gate, he was so exhausted, and his tongue so frozen by terror, he could not cry out for his family to open up the front door. Nor could he stop running.

Guandang! What a noise! He smashed right into the door, splitting the bar that fastened the two panels from within.

When his family lit the oil lamp, they found him lying facedown on the floor. They gently turned him over; his eyes had rolled up to show the whites, and foam issued from the corners of his mouth. His old body shook violently, quaking from a cold that could not be dispelled.

After his convulsions had stopped, they lifted him off the floor and laid him on the kang. They boiled ginger and fed him the broth. In time, his breath came to flow more evenly.

In the wee hours of the morning, Carpenter Wang awakened, and in a frail, brittle voice, he recounted his misadventure.

"I . . . I met my match on Badaohaodao . . ." were his last words before he lost consciousness again.

The man died at dawn. His folk buried him in the family plot. Each year, on Qingming Festival, they swept around his grave and removed the weeds growing at its base.

The sudden lament of wolves in the direction of the river worked Baba's scalp. But his cousin took no notice; he continued his hushed narrative in the back garden under the stars:

"... so nearly twenty years ago, a man named Dong Gar, who had black skin and, some thought, black blood flowing through his veins, died as he defended Shantuozi against redbeards.

"Because he had no family to keep his memory alive, folk quickly forgot about the young man's service to the village. No one swept his grave, and eventually the wind washed all traces of it away. For this treachery, this ingratitude, Dong Gar haunted Badaohaodao, to steal the souls of travelers. It was he who snatched away the life of old Carpenter Wang.

"Tonight we burned spirit money and incense along Badaohaodao, for it is Ghost Festival—the fifteenth day of the Seventh Month—and we must remember to comfort the homeless ones."

"THE OLD MAN IS breathing his last! Send one of your grandsons!" cried a harbinger of bad tidings at the House of Yang in Xinmin. "Please hurry!" The young man's chest heaved from his speedy journey. It was late one afternoon in Xinmin, during a season when light and color flow quietly out of the sky and trees and seep into the hardening earth.

"Number Four," said the Patriarch, slowly nodding to Baba—the grandson who he knew grew the most inquisitive eyes and ears upon his young head. "You must go at once to represent the fifth generation of the Yang Clan, for that branch has no one so young." The old gentleman appeared almost unmoved by the news of his relative's closeness to death; no furrow of loss dug into his handsome brow.

So it came to be that my father was recruited to take part in the "big white celebration"—the funeral ceremony—of his third great-great-grandfather, which, according to the custom of the wealthy, would last forty-nine days.

Baba's feet crushed the scuttling leaves that curled upon themselves like clenched fists, those under the eaves and the corners of walls, still frosted white.

"Persimmons! Come one, come all! Bite into this season's sweetest persimmons!" called a vendor from the street corner, peddling the bright orange fruit on the bed of his wheelbarrow. "The last harvest of the year! It'll make your tongues curl and your eyeballs roll!"

Baba did not have time for treats. He ran all the way to the house of his clansmen, who shared a common ancestor with his own folk eight generations back. He arrived, wanting of breath, in Third Great-Great-Grandfather's chamber; but the old man's bedside was so packed with sons, daughters, grandchildren, relatives, and important visitors, Baba was barely able to squeeze in a look. He knew the man would not be allowed solitude; no, there was no privacy in a big household, even in dying.

He's probably far too weak to tell everyone

to go away, Baba guessed; to say, "No, I've changed my mind; I don't want a big, noisy send-off. Leave me be and in peace!"

Blood was still pumping through the old man's body, but already the women with their flurry of arms and legs were dressing him for his journey to the netherworld. It was easier for them to dress him now than when his limbs had stiffened and hot towels would have to be applied.

The man would be attired in a robe of black brocade, with a crane flying over waves, embroidered in gold, upon the breast. Pressed upon his head, which lay shrunken on the pillow like last season's fruit, was a boat-shaped black cap with a bright red tassel at its peak. Both gown and cap were insignia of a Manchu official, for although Third Great-Great-Grandfather had never achieved an exalted position under the last emperor, it was perfectly within bounds for him to indulge his craving for honor and power in Heaven.

"*Bie ku, bie ku.* It is not time for tears,

woman. No, not yet," someone said. "Bad luck to cry now: tears will make it hard for his soul to go." Luck figured prominently in a person's death as it did throughout his life; even the women who worked to dress him had been carefully chosen: certainly no one who might carry a jinx was allowed to lay her hands upon the dying man.

When the long-expected words "*Yanqile!* He no longer breathes!" were echoed by those at the bedside, then the real and pretend tears began in earnest. The typhoon of sobbing and wailing whipped around in the chamber, against the four walls, lashed against the ceiling, and blasted into Baba's ears. There was no pause, no reflective silence. The spin of activities only grew more delirious.

Baba glimpsed a talisman, a small fish carved from green jade, as it was being placed inside the dead man's mouth; this was to ensure prosperity in the next world, for *yu*—fish—was a homonym of *yu*—abundance. Once the object was inserted, the body was snatched off the kang (as according to tradition, the son lifted the head) and removed to rest upon the bier—two door panels, supported at both ends by long wooden benches. The cooling body, already taking on a cumbrous stiffness, was then shrouded in white.

The Imperial Almanac was consulted and the exact date and time of passing looked up within its learned pages, to locate the position of the dead man's last breath.

"The vapor has reached a height of three feet and hovers to the southwest," a family member announced with scientific certitude. "It now rests near the second tier of the windows. Those panes must remain closed for the next forty-nine days."

Meanwhile, all around, there was the noise of the cutting and rending of bolts of coarse white sackcloth for the hurried tailoring of loose mourning robes, tied at the waist with ropes of hemp. Hats made from folded cloth, resembling those worn by the Daoists, covered the heads of the mourners.

An aunt brusquely fitted a hat stitched with two tiny colored squares of cloth, red and blue,

onto Baba's head, the adornments indicating his generational rank as a great-great-grandson of the deceased.

In the meantime, the eldest son had lost no time in climbing up to the rooftop on a ladder, and he could now be heard crowing instructions to the dead:

"Baba-yaaah! O Father-yaaah! Make your way to the west! Make your way to Heaven—to the Western Paradise!"

Once down from the roof, he headed a procession of four males, representatives of the four descendant generations of the Yang Clan. They wended their way to the local Tudi temple, where the Tudi Gonggong and the Tudi Nainai, the neighborhood god and his wife, awaited the death report.

The Tudi god, who maintained the register of inhabitants in his small domain, would be responsible for guiding the soul to the underworld; there it would have audience with Yanluowang, one of the judges of Hell—a bureaucrat holding office on the first level of the underworld. With the assistance of his ministers, he would either commit the soul to the lower levels of Hell for further punishments or reward it for a life of saintly conduct, allowing it to leave behind misery and woe forevermore and float in a vapor of clouds up to Heaven.

Each of the four representatives bore lighted incense as offering. Neighbors lined the way to gawk and to critique the correctness of the mourners' carriage.

"Baba-yaaah, ha ha! O Daddy-yaaah, ha ha!" the son keened at the head of the procession; but he did not put much feeling into his performance. Perhaps it was because he himself was bowing with age and saw, fast approaching, the specter of his own turn upon the bier.

"Yeye-yaaah, ha ha! O Granddaddy-yaaah, ha ha!" the grandson cried, with even less passion, following his father's recital.

"Taiye-yaaah, ha ha! O Great-Granddaddy-yaaah, ha ha!" keened the great-grandson.

Back at the house earlier on, Baba had been instructed by relatives:

"Now, run along after your elders, and when it's your turn, cry: 'Zutaiye-yaaah, ha ha!' Show proper respect: hang your head; don't lift your face up, whatever you do. Don't make the Yang Clan the laughingstock of the entire city."

So when it came time for him to keen at the end of the line, Baba cried: "Zutaiye-yaaah, ha ha! O Great-Great-Granddaddy-yaaah, ha ha!"

What tears could they possibly have expected from him?—he had absolutely no fond memories to draw his sentiments forth. He had had only the privilege of falling upon his knees in reverential kowtows at the old man's feet on New Year's Day.

In this manner, the four mourners keened repeatedly until they arrived at the miniature Tudi temple of gray bricks and tile. It had arched windows to either side of an arched door. The top of its roof rose to Baba's chest.

The centuries of incense smoke had painted the interior as lightless as the inside of a black velvet sack. Whether Tudi Gonggong and Tudi Nainai were originally sculpted from clay or wood, Baba could no longer tell. Which black lump was the god and which his wife was indicated only by the two wings that extended from the god's headdress. Only the vague protrusions that were their noses could be made out and the geography of the rest of their faces imagined in reference to them.

When his turn arrived, Baba also kowtowed before the pair of venerable black lumps and placed his bundle of incense in the urn, overflowing with ash.

They continued to report to the Tudi temple three times a day (venturing forth with lanterns at night) for the next seven days.

On the second day of the man's passing, the big white celebration began in earnest. A sizable tent of sorghum mats materialized to house the casket. The *fengshui* man, the geomancer, indicated the proper placement of the casket and divined the propitious hour that the body should be laid to rest inside the vessel of red lacquer, painted with fancy arabesques of gold. Crafted from expensive slabs of pine from the legendary

Changbai Mountain of Manchuria, it tapered toward the foot and narrowed at the base.

At the front gate, two teams of musicians from rival companies took turns squeezing music out of their horns, trying to outdo one another in repertoire and gusto. They announced the arrival of guests, who brought strings of spirit money in the form of coins or bullion.

Soon to make an appearance inside the tent were twenty-one Buddhist monks. The head monk was dressed in black, the rest in gray. Scarlet *jiasha,* strips of embroidered silk cloth, the gold threads glinting in the candlelight, were draped from their shoulders and across their chests; the head priest wore the most glittering and expensive *jiasha* of all.

Some two dozen Daoist priests, waving long horsehair whisks and attired in black brocade robes applied with the eight mystic trigrams and the yin-yang, also came with prayers upon their lips.

Baba, along with two cousins, knelt upon sorghum mats at the foot of the casket, returning the kowtows that dignitaries and friends had come to bestow upon the deceased; the visitors prostrated themselves before the soul tablet, which was placed upon the offering table laden with fruit, at the head of the casket.

"Hai, how much longer can all this kowtowing go on! The procession of visitors is endless, and my forehead is as tender as a bruised melon," Baba silently complained.

But troops of friends and relatives succeeded one another like an endless thread that would not break, for a funeral, akin to a wedding—the "big red celebration"—presented an opportunity to "eat big, drink big," and catch up on gossip. There would be no rest for Baba.

At midnight, the most elaborate of the soul masses began under the tent. The head monk sat high upon a platform situated at the head of a long table lined with rows of snowy candles that gave off good white light; he recited the sutras while ten junior monks sat to each side of the table singing hymns, striking wooden fishes, clapping cymbals, blowing upon the pipelike

sheng, and lightly tapping the *qing,* a bell-like instrument that cleared one's head and unclouded one's eyes like a crisp, cool breeze.

At this time, the steel fasteners known as "longevity nails" (Ha! What good will "longevity" do for the dead man now? Baba thought) were pounded into the lid to seal in the corpse.

The entire family knelt before the casket in postures of prayer, but each person was engrossed in his own private thoughts—desires advancing, each on its own dusty road, fearing to converge—for the passing of their elder would certainly shift the pecking order in the household, and the nebulous ties between them all would meet with more than a little tugging and pulling in the adjustments to come. The house has become too big and cumbrous, some may have been thinking. It's time to divvy up the goods. I want to strike out on my own.

The neighbors also attended in full force during this elaborate evening rite, for the music of the monks, although indecipherable to the layman, was no less ethereal than what one would expect to hear in the far reaches of Heaven.

And the neighbors came for another reason: to inspect the womenfolk of the Yang Clan, members of the household usually cloistered behind the tall walls of the compound.

Earlier that evening, a granddaughter had circled the coffin eighteen times; with each spin around the vessel, she sang her filial songs of lament. The comeliest woman was usually chosen to perform this duty.

One granddaughter-in-law, attired in simple white sackcloth, was revealed to be even more appealing without the distraction of ornaments and color: shy of her own splendor, her clean and translucent skin blushed a pale rose. It was a unanimous verdict that she was lovelier than had been rumored.

After the day's third and last soul mass, the monks departed, to partake in their vegetarian meal and then to rest. The show was now over, and the invited guests and uninvited oglers returned to their respective nests. But because Baba

was the youngest, it fell to him to watch over the casket. Others had also been assigned to the task, but they said to him:

"Number Four, you stay here for just a bit. We'll be back as soon as we take care of a few matters." They never returned, and Baba was left all alone for the wake. It was his duty to keep the candles and incense lighted and to replace them with fresh ones when they burned low.

It had all been an engrossing spectacle when the building had swelled with music and ceremony. But now the cavernous enclosure revealed an altogether different disposition.

The burdened hush of the night wandered in, bringing secrets of the dark. In the silence, it was almost as if he could hear the frost descending upon the roofs in careful layers. But to yank the collar of the jacket higher up around his neck and the sleeves down below his fingers was futile against the cold that gnawed on him from inside his chest.

The autumn wind seeped in to flutter the

expansive scrolls that hung down from the ceiling, each depicting one of the ten levels of Hell; it rippled the countless white banners whose poetry, brushed in black by famous calligraphers, eulogized the dead. The two remaining candles on the offering table trembled and threw Baba's own startling shadows across the paintings.

The more he studied the depictions of Hell, the more hugely and horribly real the images grew, the boundaries of the scrolls quietly merging with that of his own three-dimensional, concrete world; shivers jiggled the tiny hairs of his skin and caused his scalp to lift and contract, lift and contract.

In one scroll, a man was shown pierced and hung by the hook of a big balance scale: in his long, sinful life, he had thought nothing of altering the weights of the instrument to shortchange his customers.

Many a time over the course of the interminable night, the entire shelter shuddered with a strange vehemence, and the ties that lashed the sorghum mats to the frame groaned as they rubbed against the wood. The very casket seemed to rumble and shake.

"Was Third Great-Great-Grandfather deceitful in his life? Is he now hooked between the shoulder blades?" Baba wondered.

And when the wind blew even harder and the tent keened yet more ominously, the ponderous lid of the casket seemed to shift and slowly lift. His heart was pierced deep by icicles.

Now, when a man falls sick, friends and relatives feverishly pray to Heaven and Earth for his return to vigor; conversely, when a man is dead, no friend or relative would wish the corpse to step out and strut about again. Baba now prayed fervently for the deceased to remain at rest.

"Is Third Great-Great-Grandfather being tortured in Hell? Maybe he can't take it anymore and is trying to crawl back out!" he thought out loud.

"I don't think he likes it much in the casket now. . . . I heard he used to try it out for comfort and size when he was still quite spry, taking a lot of pride in the costly box that would one day encase him."

Baba wrenched his focus back to the images of Hell, for it was more restful for his heart to study these than the lid of the casket. He was repelled but, at the same time, entranced by the dazzling (albeit gruesome) artistry. Human souls were tossed upon crags of gleaming knives by swarthy redheaded devils, whose nostrils flared as big and round as those of horses: punishment for those who had gained their daily bowls of rice by bloodshed. Others were driven with pitchforks into vats of oil and deep fried: these had been unfilial sons and daughters. Spiky "wolf fang" cudgels ripped into the naked flesh of those who had committed the unredeemable crime of grave desecration. Demons gouged out the eyes of those who had snooped on their friends and neighbors. Baba checked to see that his own soft, pink tongue was rooted solidly in his head as devils sliced out those of folk whose Buddha-like words had concealed snake hearts. His eyes finally came to rest upon the wheel of reincar-

nation in the tenth and last painting: souls not allowed to waft heavenward but spat back upon the earth as cows, chickens, mules, or poor, suffering man.

"I wonder if Great-Great-Grandfather is being changed into a rooster or a dog?" Baba wondered.

Not only the sights and sounds of the night were disturbing; his sense of smell was assaulted by the insidious combination of pine, lacquer, incense, candle wax, oily smoke from the burning of the paper spirit money, and the sacramental sorghum wine. No, there was no putrid odor of a corpse: the season was chill, and the body had been placed inside a separate case within the casket, the lid of each vessel sealed tight with putty; but nonetheless the essence of death hung thick and black down from the ceiling about his ears, entered his nose, and settled with an astringency in his throat.

Yet the morrow did finally arrive for Baba; it swept away all the evil, bringing far more cheerful visions to his eyes and a taste of sunlight upon his tongue.

On that third day of mourning, in an empty streetside lot, with the neighbors watching and their wild children skipping about, colorful and delicately crafted models of houses (and everything contained inside, including the bedding), along with miniature barnyard animals, were set on fire, sending everything in a happy blaze up into the sky. All the household effects were now ready for Third Great-Great-Grandfather when he would arrive at his new home in the sky. Everything he had possessed in his life on earth would be available to him in Heaven (provided that he did make it to that hallowed address and was not returned home from the netherworld as the sacrificial Spring Festival pig).

"No paper cow to be burned this time," Baba said to himself. "Big thirsty cows are for women . . . like when neighbor Ding's wife died and they provided her with one in the afterlife so that it would drink up all the water—all the water she may have wasted in her lifetime of cooking and cleaning."

After the seventh day, the tent was taken down and the feasting drew to an end, but every seven days thereafter, Buddhist monks returned to conduct a quieter soul mass at noon in the smaller shelter that came to protect the casket.

But the most colorful and noisy part of the big white celebration was yet to come.

On the forty-ninth day, the last day of mourning, under a shattering blue sky, the coffin was carried aloft upon a spacious palanquin in the shape of a house. The indigo cloth was embroidered with dragons swirling among clouds and the figures of two children, "Golden Boy" and "Jade Girl," who would provide gentle escort to the deceased on his journey to Heaven.

The palanquin was borne on the shoulders of sixteen highly trained, uniformed pallbearers in conical hats that looked like blue lampshades. Their leader scrambled about all around them and sometimes rode in the palanquin itself, peering out the tiny window at the front; he directed them in their precise stepping by the variations in the *clack-clack-clack*ing of his two batons, shiny with use, made from the wood of the "steel plum" tree. When signaled, the pallbearers responded flawlessly, like marchers in a military band; they knew exactly when those in the rear should take two side steps for every step taken by those up at the front, in order to swing the palanquin around. Negotiating some of the narrow streets and alleys was no easy matter: the vehicle was some fifteen feet long by eight feet wide, and those in back were blinded by its sheer size.

At the very head of the cavalcade cavorted three leering, wide-mouthed *kailugui*—devils who clear the way—men whose faces were painted blue and green in the manner of demons, to frighten away the multitudes who had gathered to take in the sights, jamming the streets so hopelessly as to force the procession to a complete halt.

Trailing the "devils" came a pair of gongs—each carried upon a shoulder pole between two men—their deep, dull *kwwooonng* chased by the discord of horns and cymbals. And directly behind the costumed musicians came a swirl of Buddhists and the Daoists in their cascading robes, kicking up pale yellow dust. Last of all, stringing along behind the palanquin itself, drifted the endless procession of resolute mourners in sackcloth (the women riding in horse-drawn carts), generations following upon generations, bearing the fluttering white funeral banners.

Traipsing along near the very end of the procession was Baba. "Look at that one there," he overheard an onlooker, elbowing for a better view, say to her companion. "That grieving one over there, she's got her handkerchief held over her mouth and she's moanin', but she ain't really foolin' no one!"

"Now look at that ancient woman there, though. She's an old hand at this; she's got the crying down to an art . . . does the dead man proud," said another backseat mourner.

But in general, folk along the way sighed with great envy and admiration at the procession and were unanimous in the verdict that the corpse was more elegant than had been rumored.

Third Great-Great-Grandfather's branch of the Yang Clan had grown immensely prosperous over the years, and so it had come to establish its own family burial grounds in Xinmin instead of upon Old Granddaddy Hill in the ancestral village of Shantuozi.

It was a big plot, in the sparsely populated northern reaches of town. Mounds stood to mark the existing graves. Young cypresses and willows had been newly planted on the grounds.

With somber ceremony, the casket was lowered into the grave. The eldest son shoveled a few spadefuls of dirt and then kowtowed, his brittle old bones creaking. Buddhist monks circled and muttered prayers. Cymbals crashed to the whine of the dozens of trumpets as workmen labored to fill the grave. Later, a circular brick enclosure would wrap around the loose mound of dirt and a slab of stone carved with the man's illustrious name would stand in front of it.

And thus ended the big white celebration, a ceremony whose rituals had once, long ago, held deep meaning for the mourners but had over the course of the millennia become numb showmanship.

The elaborate funeral of Third Great-Great-Grandfather had lasted forty-nine days and consumed a great deal of money; but the man of wealth had died happy in the dream that every year, filial descendants would come to sweep around his grave, pick the weeds, and sing his praise.

At the time of Third Great-Great-Grandfather's death—while the star of the Yang Clan was still ascendant—another clan, the Lis of Xinmin, were seeing their prosperous days dwindle into a sullen darkness. Though their name still rang with respect, it was but a hollow echo of their former authority.

At the House of Yang, in the study of the Patriarch, there hung a scroll, the calligraphy upon it brushed by the sure hand of the clan's most notable Li. Li Rubai—Plum That Is as Cypress—was the man's highly poetic name. Baba loved to study the gracious, yet resolute, script of a man who had passed away long before his own emergence into the world.

It was said that Li Rubai had served in a high office in the last dynasty and returned from Beijing to retire with vast stores of riches. The man held court in Xinmin, living within an immense compound with two sets of imposing vermilion gates. The unplanted area of the grounds was entirely paved in gray brick, and in the outer courtyard stood an exquisite platform built from gleaming white stones, on which the aged former official, assisted by his servants, stood to mount and dismount his horses.

But because of the luxurious life his wealth afforded the generations that followed him, his sons, grandsons, and great-grandsons invested no shadow of a thought in the making of money, but instead planned their clement days around the spending of it. They idled away the hours wearing extravagant clothes and indulging their individual vices.

Some took up the expensive hobby of raising rare species of songbirds; Baba had often seen Li Rubai's great-grandsons tote ornate cages, which they would carry in pairs, hanging from hooks at the ends of dainty, carved shoulder poles. At the edge of town, in a pine forest brushed by a breeze, they joined with other bird fanciers to lift the cages high in the air, thereby coaxing their birds into bursts of song.

But with no love for labor instilled in the hearts of his descendants, it was natural that the fortune of Li Rubai should slip away in time, and naturally this process was accelerated after the death of the man.

It was easy for the folk of Xinmin to read the telltale signs of decline at the House of Li. The main gate, when money had been plentiful, was scrupulously maintained every year with shiny coats of vermilion paint; but when the coffers grew shallow, the paint was allowed to fade, crack, and peel, and later to exfoliate in unsightly layers like severely sunburned skin.

In the ensuing years, the walls surrounding the compound came tumbling down. Initially, the descendants of Li Rubai sold only the scattered bricks, but in time they themselves tore down the still-standing sections, selling it all. Once the walls were gone, needless to say, there was no more use for the gates, so these, in their turn, were pulled down and the materials sold.

What was left standing were only the buildings—solitary, naked, and shrunken into themselves, the window frames puckered from the elements, looking like eyes averted in shame.

One day in the summer following Third Great-Great-Grandfather's death, Baba overheard the grown-ups gossiping in the North Garden at home.

"Those descendants of Li Rubai, they're good-for-nothings," said an aunt.

"Why so?" asked an uncle.

"Well, now that they've sold everything, including the buildings, they're digging up the graves in the ancestral burial grounds. And do you know how they reason it to the neighbors? They say the site has proved to be unlucky: the *fengshui*—wind and water—is bad, and this is why their great fortune has come to nothing.

They say they will remove the bones to somewhere with improved *fengshui*.

"It's all very thinly veiled. Hunnh! You know as well as I do, they've been reduced to grave robbing. Desecration! Better to pillage your own family than to let strangers do it for you later!"

Ever eager for the unusual, Baba on that day took it upon himself to see how the task of emptying ancestral graves was done. He came to the burial grounds of the House of Li, in the northwest section of town.

Generations of the Lis had been buried here, so it was no small task to raise all the resting bones.

Big-bellied ceramic urns, which came up to Baba's own belly, stood next to the graves to be excavated. The narrow openings of the vessels were covered with pieces of red cloth, and each urn was marked with the name of the ancestor whose crumbling femurs and clavicles would be placed inside it.

Ceremony was still needed to maintain face

before the noisy crowd that had gathered. A solitary musician had been hired to blow his tinny horn. A few bowls of uncooked sorghum and soybeans held sticks of lighted incense. A few hurried kowtows were made to the long-departed spirits.

As the trumpet played on, Baba watched the men pry open the disintegrating casket of Li Rubai himself and go grubbing inside.

Termites had chewed through the wood. Baba guessed that ants had also taken up residence, from the strong scent the insects gave off. The inside was revealed to be filled with dirt.

Li Rubai's skull was first removed from the rubble and slotted through the opening of the urn. Baba heard it land on the bottom with a dry clatter. The larger leg and hip bones were withdrawn to the urn also, but the small, broken, or loose pieces were left to continue their slow transformation into dust.

But bones, of course, were not what the descendants of Li Rubai had come for.

They rooted for the antiques and valuables that the man had loved in his life and that had been interred with him. Once the larger objects had been lifted out, they sifted long and hard for the small jade and gold pieces that were customarily placed in or over the "seven orifices": the eyes, the ears, the nose, and the mouth of the dead.

Baba saw a small fish carved in green jade removed from the dirt and placed in one of the waiting cloth sacks—not in the urn.

This jade fish is just like the one that I saw placed in Third-Great-Great-Grandfather's mouth, thought Baba. No doubt this piece was once set upon the tongue of Li Rubai himself.

In the casket of Li Rubai's wife, the descendants painstakingly strained for gold, silver, and precious jewels in the form of head ornaments, necklaces, bangles, and rings.

"You know, the grandsons and great-grandsons are extravagantly rich again," it was later widely rumored throughout Xinmin. "Do you realize how many generations of Lis were buried there! Think of the hoard!"

But Baba wondered: What will ultimately happen to the bones in the urns? Yet there was no need for him to inquire; it was an easy guess that the bones of the great ancestors would be taken to the wilds, far outside town—a place similar to the desolation of Badaohaodao in distant Shantuozi—where homeless beggars were customarily buried, wrapped only in reed mats. Thrown into shallow holes in the lonely no-man's-land, wrapped only in the hush of dust and stones, the bones of the Li Clan were to be laid to final rest.

Within a few years, even the ancestral burial grounds would be parceled out and sold; the cypresses would be cut down and carted away for firewood.

"I have studied the sacred *I Ching*—the *Book of Changes*—for a decade now, burning many a tall candle late into the night . . . ," Baba read from his beloved scroll in the Patriarch's study.

It was the evening of my father's return from the excavations of the Li Clan. Suddenly a deeper meaning had surfaced from the familiar calligraphy. He read on:

". . . With my growing understanding of the *I Ching,* the brush in my hand has come to be charged with the mighty, limitless spirit of the never constant, ever changing universe. Signed, Li Rubai from West of the river Liao."

The brilliant brushwork in "running script," each character's stance like that of a proud man standing with arms folded behind him, flowed in quiet confidence upon the wall. The scroll was a personal gift to the thriving Yang Clan from Li himself—he who had perhaps in his lifetime learned to relinquish the mortal dream of everlasting prosperity.

MY FATHER'S THIRD grandaunt had only heard about fire wagons. She had never seen one. The north-south railroad line running from Shenyang to Beiping had been in existence for decades, but it did not rumble through her village.

"Fire wagons . . . fire wagons," Baba heard her say at the House of Yang. "How queer for a wagon to run on flames." She knew wheelbarrows, cow wagons, donkey carts, and horse carts, but a fire wagon was something beyond the bubble of her world and imagination.

She had never ventured outside her native village of Shantuozi. When she came to Xinmin to attend the big white celebration, the funeral ceremony of her clansman, it was the first time she had traveled the sixty li—a day's journey by wagon—to the neighboring city.

Women—and especially country women like her—had few opportunities for adventure, however mild: they were made busy holding up more than their half of the world.

As girls, they were kept within the narrow confines of their homes, feeding the geese, goats, pigs, and chickens; sewing clothes; embroidering; making shoes. It was improper for unmarried young women to be perused by strangers on the streets.

As they grew older, opportunities to venture out came even more rarely, for after they married, their time was taken up entirely by cooking, washing, waiting on the husbands and the in-laws, and raising the bumper crops of children. Only when they reached old age, when they had daughters-in-law themselves to do the tedious chores, did they merit attendance at weddings and funerals of relatives in distant places.

Third Grandauntie was short and plump and walked with the curious hip sway of women with miniaturized feet (they were liberated from the bandages used for foot-binding when she was already an adult). Baba always heard her laughing and giggling, for as a matriarch of nearly seventy with a troop of daughters-in-law (and an army of grandchildren), she had little to worry her soul.

"Third Grandauntie, if you'd like, I can take you to the station to see the fire wagons for yourself," Baba heard Second Brother say.

Elder Brother, standing next to Baba, groaned. He considered himself a scholar and had no time for such nonsense.

Nainai shot a worried look in her second son's direction, as she puffed silently on her long-stemmed pipe.

"Take me along too! I've never seen a fire wagon either," said a bent old matron from the country.

"Nor I," echoed another.

Only Second Brother, his soul as deep and wide as the Yellow Sea, would think to play tour guide to gammers from the countryside. He was an athletic, companionable fellow; a man with a toothy grin and lots of laughter. Everyone liked him.

They began their outing at eight o'clock the following morning. Second Brother, like a hefty mother hen, had half a dozen cheerful, chirping ladies—hair up in slicked-back, neat little buns—trailing him to the train station across town.

They arrived with only a few minutes to spare. The once-a-day southbound train from Shenyang "galloped and reared in, belching smoke," as Third Grandauntie described it.

"I'll buy everyone a platform ticket. Then all you ladies can get a closer look," said Second Brother. "It'll be much better than craning your necks from this waiting room window."

The train slowed to a stop.

"Aiyaya! *Mrrr, mrrr, mrrr*—it cries as loud as ten cows, but it is ten thousand times bigger," said Grandauntie as she gazed upon the beast, her toothless mouth sprung open.

"They've come so far . . . why not let them have a look inside," said Second Brother to himself. He boosted his brood, one by one, into the nearest passenger car.

"Hai, how elegant! How lovely!" They sighed and twittered. They ran their hands along the backs of the shiny black vinyl seats, touched the starched green tablecloths, and fingered the porcelain vases adorned with silk flowers. It was like nothing they'd ever seen back home.

As Second Brother tried to school them toward the rear exit, the train began to pull out of the station.

"Hurry! Hurry! Please go quickly! We must get off!" he cried; but his charges, twisting and swiveling on their tiny feet, could not shift any faster.

"Aiya! We're moving," said one delighted grandma.

"Yes, sister, we most certainly are. There's no lurching at all—the ride is smoother than the horse carts with the newfangled rubber tires," said Third Grandauntie.

Second Brother was sweating like a rain cloud. "I only paid for platform tickets. Now I've no more money, and we're on our way to Beiping. . . . What am I going to tell the folks back home? . . . If we ever manage to get back home."

"This is strange. Number Two Son has been gone with the womenfolk since morning," said Yeye at the House of Yang. Baba saw that his father's face was ashen. "We sent Number Four and the wagoner to bring them all home, but they were not to be found. There was no sign of them anywhere. How could that be? It isn't as if we're searching for one lost needle." Yeye liked life orderly and without surprises.

"Only Number Two would be softheaded enough to take them. Only he could manage to lose them all—and himself in the bargain," Eldest Brother said with a sneer.

"I was afraid something just like this would occur," said Nainai. "Aiya, to have a worrisome son like this Number Two. On the day I was born, hail the size of duck eggs descended from the sky; this, the seers said to my mother, would mean that I would be living life as a series of unfolding disasters. Hunnh, how right they were. Why, it was just last winter that Number Two—that bad egg—brought me so much trouble. Do you all remember what happened?!"

How could Baba forget? Rarely had he seen his mother so angry.

His second, and favorite, of four brothers, older by six years, loved food. Good food. Once he was old enough to hold a job, he went to work as an accountant for Xinmin County. He could then afford to leave behind the jostling dinner table, the dueling chopsticks, and the unappealing food cooked in bulk to feed a large family.

Nattily attired in a Western suit and sporting a tweed cap, he frequented the restaurants that catered mouthwatering delicacies such as "lion's head," "pork potstickers with silver ears," and "mutton hot pot."

Baba was envious of his brother, for he was still young and had to eat at home. In the winter, when he helped his brother on with his heavy winter coat, he was allowed to fish in the pocket for loose coins with which to buy morsels of roasted donkey meat; the sinewy flesh above the hoof of the unfortunate beast was all he could afford. But more often, he shadowed Second Brother to the restaurants, to be fed for the price of not tattling on the elder's indulgence.

The previous year, his brother had outspent his meager income but continued to patronize his favorite eateries, charging the bills to the county government.

Of course, the county would not pay for his excess. At the end of the year, when all obligations had to be met, he was faced with the prospect of spending Spring Festival, the Chinese New Year, in debtors' prison.

"Wife, how will we pay the bill for Number Two's big appetite? I have no income of my own," Yeye had said to Nainai. "Now you must return to your mother's house and sell your cattle. How else to rescue him? We cannot ask the Patriarch for the money, for the other family members will surely look on red-eyed and make a big fuss. Ah, you must go quickly, to save the face of the House of Yang."

When Nainai was a girl, she had earned money by gleaning the soybean fields after harvest. She had saved to buy a cow; later on, when she had more money, she bought the solitary cow a mate. Not surprisingly, left to themselves, the animals reproduced.

Nainai's nephew had been charged with the care of the herd when she married.

Over the busy years, as a daughter-in-law whose days revolved around the hot kitchen stove at the House of Yang, she thought of her cattle only rarely, but now, confronted with selling them, Nainai was reminded of how hard she had worked as a girl to acquire them; it did not please her in the least to sacrifice her animals to save her spendthrift son.

Nainai traveled in the back of a mule-drawn wagon in the snow for the two-day journey to her mother's house in the country; there she compelled her nephew to drive five head of cattle to market.

The nephew did so with great reluctance, for since her marriage, his aunt had never made mention of her property; he had been hoping that she had forgotten about them entirely. Besides, her cattle had bred with his and multiplied, and now no one had a clear account of which animals belonged to whom.

"Since the sale had to take place in such a big hurry," the nephew said to Nainai, "I was only able to sell two cattle out of the five." (Perhaps, at market, he had simply decided to part with only two.)

"And they sold at a very bad price," the nephew added. (Perhaps, at home, he had simply decided to hand over the money for only one.)

"Never mind," Nainai said when she heard the bad news. "I must get back to Xinmin quickly."

She returned, braving the snow, just in the nick of time to save Baba's second brother from the jailer.

The winter sun slid rapidly down into the west as the family waited and waited with mounting alarm and anger, imagining all sorts of tragic ends.

When, finally, Baba was pressed once again to search at the train station, he heard the dogs barking at the gate and peals of laughter just outside.

"I'm so hungry, I can eat an entire roast pig

by myself," came the voice of Third Grand-auntie, who was leading the pack of tired but happy women warriors; not a single strand of her hair had come loose from her tight little bun.

"We went all the way to Willow Creek Vil-lage! In less than half an hour, we traveled twenty-five li!" explained Grandauntie to Baba between giggles. "We had to wait the entire afternoon to return on another fire wagon. We had no money for the tickets . . . but Number Two convinced them that the House of Yang would most certainly take care of the bill later."

Second Brother, who was bringing up the rear, smiled sheepishly.

"Out the windows, I saw the trees and poles, the mules and dogs, run backward!" continued my father's third grandauntie. "Can you imagine that . . . can you just imagine! The world goes by different rules outside of my home in Shantuozi."

SQUATTING SOME distance to the northwest of my father's hometown of Xinmin was a section of an old wall; centuries ago, when it held itself taller, it served as a formidable barrier against the nomadic tribes of the steppe. Once the Manchu hordes had broken across in the 1600s to begin their reign over the Middle Kingdom, it fell into ruin; what remained in Baba's time was only a bank of dirt—sculpted round and smooth as only the hands of time can do—testament to a past of bloodshed, rapid-fire beating of hearts, and the roar of cannons upon the terraces.

Ages ago, a village had grown up along a point near the old wall and derived its name, Dongpaotaizi, from its proximity to the Eastern Cannon Terrace. But in time, folk simply came to call it Puotaizi, Broken Terrace.

Now, in the year Baba turned fifteen, the wagoner at the House of Yang told him a story about a personage who had once inhabited this village. The old man had borne the very lofty epithet of Zhao the Juren. But how he had come

to acquire that imperial title was a question that had rubbed in everyone's mind. It was not known that he had taken the many examinations to attain that elevated office under the Emperor. It was guessed (for the man would never have admitted to this) that he had, at great expense, bought the title when the days of the Qing began to segue into dusk—when the dynasty of the Manchus was on its last legs and was hard up for cash.

But if, indeed, he did buy the title, how did Zhao come up with the money in the first place? No one had been certain on this point either.

"Just as a horse doesn't fatten up unless given extra feed in the night," folk were wont to comment, "a man's purse doesn't fatten up without goods derived in the murky darkness."

And the rumors in and around Broken Terrace were elaborated over time like fancy embroidery:

It was said that Zhao and his wife began life together in a mud cottage, where, upon moving in, they discovered that in the evening, out of a corner of their hut, a strange froglike creature with only three legs would come hopping out, its body glowing gold in the dark. When they tried to catch it, the critter hop-skipped back into the corner. The wife of Zhao then removed a long bronze hairpin from her bun and gave it a stab, and the three-legged thing vanished like a firefly when it snuffs out its light. But as soon as she removed the pin from the corner, the creature came hopping back out again.

"This must be a sign from Heaven: there's got to be something buried here," Zhao said to his wife. When the shine of the moon no longer rapped against their windowpanes, and the only sound was the nibbling of the mice, they began to dig. And lo and behold! their shovel struck something that rang like pottery. It turned out to be not one but three urns filled with bullion of gold.

And so this had been the talk in the neighborhood about the origin of Zhao's wealth. It was not wholly unimaginable that the couple should have come upon such a cache, for throughout the unsettled centuries on the frontier, with the ever-present threat of plundering nomads, folk made it a habit to bury their valuables. If the owners died, the secret died with them, the treasures waiting for some lucky fellows to come upon them sometime in the future.

But regardless of how Zhao had come upon the money to buy the title of *juren*, buy it he did once he had taken his family to Beijing, the capital. And as soon as this imperial title was had, it was no longer necessary for him to root for hidden treasures, if indeed that was what he had done. As was common knowledge, a title was the surest, smoothest avenue to great wealth; large sums were consistently passed under the table to an official by the long lines of supplicants knocking at his gate.

After fattening his coffer for many decades in the capital, Zhao, when retirement came, returned to Broken Terrace, bought vast tracts of land, built his big house, and hung an impressive robe of office upon his wall (most likely purchased at a pawnshop in Beijing). Back in his native village, he and his growing clan lived their days in style and comfort.

Now, it was always easy for a son of a wealthy family to marry, for it was not improper for him to wed a woman from a family less prominent than his own; yet for a daughter, it was altogether a different matter: it was crucial that she be paired to someone her social and economic equal, or, better yet, one whose family wealth and standing were superior to her own.

Many years down the line, when it came time for the only granddaughter of Zhao the Juren to marry, there was not a single fellow to be found who was able to meet the stringent requirements of her family. And had there been, it was unlikely that he would have asked for her hand, for she was undeniably unattractive.

A bulky, tub-shaped woman with tiny eyes shaped like a pair of inverted spoons, she was said by many, shaking their heads, to be the spitting image of her grandfather. Worse yet, she also had his temper, they would say, for although the granddaughter never actually struck anybody with the broom or with her grandfather's walking cane—weapons that she came to wield often—the big woman with her martial stance was intimidating to both visitors at the house and to her own family.

Though deficient in beauty and poise, the granddaughter did not lack in education, for contrary to the norm for girls, she had been tutored at home in the Confucian Classics. This only made the prospect of marriage even worse for her. According to a proverb, "Girls who are in want of talent are virtuous and bring good fortune to all"; so, conversely, girls of talent were believed to be big trouble. No man would want a wife who was too capable: the rooster, not the hen, was responsible for the crowing.

Now, many years earlier, following immediately upon the return of the *Juren* to Broken Terrace, a nun had arrived at his door, chanting the sutras and striking the ritual *qing*.

"Ah, I see that the main gate of your house faces southwest," she had said in her wise, practiced voice. "That is the direction from which the *shui* flows; this is the reason why wealth has been pouring into your house like floodwater." Yes, she knew the savory words that the rich had a special weakness for.

"Do you have a family altar to Buddha?" she had then asked. Once invited in, she said: "Ah, yes, but I see that it faces too much to the southwest. The devout *huo,* the fire of the altar, will be put out by too much *shui.* You must shift its direction slightly away to avoid calamity and to ensure continued good fortune."

And later on, when she had come to be on more familiar terms with the family, her recommendations increased:

"I've heard that up in Qian Mountain, there is a solitary monk-artist whose brush invokes the spirit of the true Buddha. To hang a painting by such a man upon your wall will surely invite the divine presence into your home and bring even greater prosperity in the generations to come." Over the years, the nun had successfully insinuated herself deep into the bosom of the

rich family: to them, her every word was holy, and naturally she came to receive large donations from them to fill her coffer.

In the year that the granddaughter of Zhao the Juren had reached her most unmarriageable fortieth birthday, the nun made her recommendation to the family:

"It is no good for her to sit at home like this. I suggest you hand her over to me, and I will lead her along the path to enlightenment." The family agreed to let the granddaughter go, for it was known to everyone that a house with an old maid was not in the least conducive to good fortune.

No one knew how the spinster agreed to this arrangement, for she did not display her usual ferocity but silently followed the nun out of the house into retreat. Her face had emptied; no dull pain rippled there. How did she come to terms with her layers of regret for the days of fulfillment that came to others as naturally as sunlight and wind?

Initially, the granddaughter—always closely watched by the nun—returned for short visits, but after a year these became infrequent, until she stopped coming home altogether and information on her whereabouts became unavailable even to her own kin.

But in the spring of 1944, as the Japanese puppet state of Manchukuo was reeling into decline, the family wagoner told Baba the curious story of the woman's return to Broken Terrace (and so, consequently, he told Baba all the rumors and lore of how her grandfather had acquired his title and wealth).

"She's been meditating deep in some mountain way up there in the province of Heilongjiang," the wagoner said. "She hid herself away in a teensy cubicle with no door—only a small opening through which food and water could be passed to her. In that world of four walls, she remained all alone for ten years. Think of it—ten years! I reckon two to three years is a great many for one to sit 'n' meditate. It's been said that she has attained enlightenment and is back in her native village. There she receives the devout who come to seek her blessing."

It seemed that the family of Zhao the Juren—the old man was long since dead—was happy to receive her back, not as a bitter old maid but as a living Buddha (as her ever-present old guardian, the nun, pronounced her).

The granddaughter was changed. Her anger had gone. And though she remained a big woman, the cumbersomeness that came with her bulk was lost and she moved with a regal, straight-limbed sureness. Some folk even ventured to say that her face came close to being beautiful in the splendor of her tranquillity. What indescribable freedom had come to her in sitting and sitting in the cell of her emancipation?

Her family built her a temple on family land, and the old nun became her mouthpiece.

The rumor of the granddaughter's divine powers rippled like wind across the plains to far-flung towns and villages. The more they talked of her powers—one person telling two, two people telling four—the greater grew her fame, and so her authority.

It was said that when the sick staggered

before her, she rubbed their heads or dispensed to them holy water from the "Heavenly River," and they were made healthy and whole again, the pain banished from their limbs.

The hale and strong also came seeking her benedictions: wagoners who delivered goods for journeys of hundreds of li across the bandit-swept grasslands came to kowtow before her feet, asking protection for man and beast.

Old parents of drovers who traveled to Inner Mongolia—over three hundred li, far outside the ancient dirt wall—there to buy cattle, asked that their men and boys be returned home safely to Manchuria: many were known to have been killed by rustlers or by angry farmers whose plantings had been eaten by herds on their way southeast.

Men and women, young and old, streamed to the temple, tramping a path upon which no green thing dared to sprout; soon they forced the Zhao family to build a wall all around to control the crowds that arrived before dawn and had to be shooed away at dusk. The more eager and agile of the suppliants clambered over the walls instead of waiting to be let in through the gate.

But two women were no longer enough to assert control over the multitudes and to maintain the temple: orphaned girls were recruited as novices to keep the candles lighted and to sweep the grounds; poor relatives of the Zhao clan found very profitable employment there, for the business of Buddhism required many able hands to gather the money that rolled in through the door.

With money from the overflowing coffer, the temple was enlarged; inner and outer courtyards came to be established with the raising of another set of walls; next to the hall of Buddha, a room was added, in which carpenters crafted a golden throne in the shape of an unfolding lotus; there, upon the petals, the granddaughter of Zhao the Juren rested as she received the river of suppliants.

But as the crowd continued to swell—the smell of bodies thickening unbearably and incense smoke stinging the eyes—the granddaugh-

ter grew physically weary of giving benedictions; she sat cross-legged upon her throne, shut her eyes, and meditated. There was to be no more rubbing of the heads. This distancing only caused her reputation to soar even higher.

"Look at her tranquil, radiant face," folk said in awe. "Her skin is as that of a child, though she's in her fifties: the rosy cheeks of a babe."

"How can she be a living Buddha?" Baba wondered during a trip to the temple with the family wagoner in late summer. "She sips tea from a dainty cup, and from a gilded dish she eats the flesh of melon seeds that others have diligently cracked for her. I thought living Buddhas had need for neither food nor water."

Others had similar doubts, and soon after Baba's visit to Broken Terrace, it was reported that the tea and melon seeds had been removed. It was also said that she now meditated day and night, never coming down off her lotus dais.

Subsequently, a solemn rumor raged: the living Buddha will be returning to the "Western Heaven"! And supplicants came to see that, instead of a rosy glow, the skin of the Buddha had come to be suffused with a golden light.

And with this fantastic revelation, countryfolk came in even greater droves, and the flood of donations to the temple became a deluge.

But though the craze over the living Buddha was widespread, not everyone was an enthusiastic believer. One particular group grew downright fearful of her. These were the Japanese authorities, whose grasp on power was ever slipping in Manchuria.

"What if she meddles in politics! What if she tries to turn these peasants against us! You know she holds the minds and hearts of the masses upon her peacefully cupped hands. The countryfolk are magnetized! They come from great distances, getting up at daybreak to make the trek, taking one step and prostrating, taking another step and prostrating; they go on for days like this, arranging to stay at inns or with relatives along the way; they continue to walk and prostrate, walk and prostrate, until they have reached her lotus throne.

"The living Buddha," the paranoid Japanese said, "may be aiding the Chinese underground to facilitate our overthrow."

So they dispatched their police to the temple at Broken Terrace, and the men upon arrival said: "We have come to protect the Buddha, seeing that the throng has become unruly."

But of course, they had come hoping to break the spell of her enchantment.

The Japanese were devout Buddhists themselves and therefore did not attempt to shut down the operation; neither did they try to bar the entry of the pilgrims into the temple.

What they did was simple: they maintained a round-the-clock vigil on the woman seated upon the lotus throne. "If this one is truly a living Buddha, as that old fox of a nun claims, she will not sully her lips with food," they said. And so they bent their eyes to her lips, making sure that the woman was not sneaked morsels in the middle of the night, when the doors of the temple were shut to the blindly worshipful.

Now, it is true that a person, through long years of self-mortification, can come to master flesh and spirit, able to meditate for days on end without stirring; so the police watched and they watched in the expanding silence.

After maintaining her posture for one day, two days, three days, four days, on the evening of the fifth day, with a loud *gudong!* that came with no introduction, the living Buddha tumbled off her lotus petals, headfirst onto the brick floor, very close to becoming a dead Buddha.

Her guardian, the old nun, pleaded with the Japanese authorities for mercy, for it was she who had masterminded the hoax; she had been the one to paint the face of her charge with rouge and later to dust it with gold powder.

The Japanese did not punish the pair (it was believed that money passed under the table) but simply told them to remove themselves from the territory. Having learned to bow toward the "no" in life, the granddaughter of Zhao the Juren vanished from Broken Terrace with the old nun, without so much as a word.

"The living Buddha has indeed returned to

the Western Heaven," Baba heard pilgrims returning from Broken Terrace say. But my father was more inclined to believe the remarks of those who sighed with envy:

"That Zhao Clan sure knows how to rake in the money. The skill and knowledge runs in the family—from granddaddy right on down to granddaughter. Hai, those who have it in their blood will sniff their way to riches no matter what."

"DEMONS WILL RISE when the realm is in decline," a very old graybeard said. "I've seen it before—I've seen it with these faint old eyes of mine. Mark my words: when rulers fall, the unnatural will fly."

And upon hearing this declaration, Baba, like folk all around him, fell into a meditative silence filled with a mixture of joy, curiosity, and fear—joy in that the illegitimate state of Manchukuo would be vanquished; curiosity about the changes that would ensue; and fear that the name of the changes would be chaos.

But such prognostications brought purely terror to the hearts of the ruling Japanese. Their nervousness over the influence of the living Buddha had been one of the many indications that their power was on the wane.

They had been in Manchuria since 1931, thirteen years now. Their strength had been in steady decline for three years, since their attack on Pearl Harbor, which had brought unequivocal American involvement in the war on the side of the Chinese.

And because they were losing their grip, the Japanese clamped down even more severely on the people. From the Manchurians was exacted a heavy load; staples like soybeans and sorghum, and cotton for clothing, were strictly rationed and sent to feed and outfit far-flung Japanese troops, fighting in the Pacific.

It was in the late autumn of 1944, after the sorghum had been harvested, that my father heard the rumors of a strange phenomenon such as the graybeard had forecast.

A short distance to the northeast of Xinmin, in a former Manchu outpost called Lanqipuzi—Garrison of the Blue Banner—a white horse had appeared with the first snowfall that blanketed the Manchurian plains.

"It is most queer," Baba heard folk declare. "It flies on its long legs like the wind, its white mane streaming. No one is able to lasso it, not even the troops of expert horsemen who ride after it."

"Some of these fellows claim to have witnessed a slice of blinding light beam down from above, into which the horse would suddenly vanish."

"Most unnatural . . ."

In that same autumn, other bizarre happenings were reported.

One evening, at the House of Yang, Baba heard from his fourth uncle about the deviant behavior of one of Xinmin's own. An old woman named Ma Po-po.

"Ai yo yo!" the old woman had cried in alarm one afternoon at the Temple to the God of Hell.

Hard-boiled eyes embedded in a green face had stared her down. The all-penetrating eyes belonged to the wooden statue of Panguan, the Supreme Judge of the Underworld, who held out the Book of Life and Death to her upon the spread of his expansive palm.

Did Ma Po-po glance upon her own name and fatal hour recorded within the pages of the tome? Did she come across the punishments that would be meted out to her for a lifetime's worth of sins?

On Panguan's right was a devil with the long face of a horse, and to his left, a demon with the meaty head of a cow; imps and hobgoblins, rattling chains, skipped about below their knees.

Folk claimed these were the last images the old woman saw before invisible claws seized her ankles and yanked her to the ground.

Her son found her sprawled unconscious on the gray-brick floor in front of the sculptures at the temple. Here was where the folk of Xinmin came to make offerings, hoping to placate the rulers of the underworld.

After her son had carried her home and set her down on the kang, her withered body curled up like a fetus and remained motionless. Healers administered medicine and witch doctors droned incantations, but none could awaken her. Her eyelids and lips were sealed tight in bitter lines.

And thus she remained until the morning of the twentieth day, when without warning she sat bolt upright, rolled her bleary old eyes, and whispered, "In a hundred days, I'll have fully become. . . ."

And all who heard her words felt their fingers and toes go cold, for they knew that a demon was what she would become.

Henceforth, the old woman refused to eat at the table with her family; instead she ate sitting cross-legged upon the kang, with a thick quilt thrown over her head, covering her entirely like a volcanic mound. Holding the emptied rice bowl, she would extend her bony forearm out from under the hump and croak, "Give us more grub!" Her appetite had become as large as that of a man in the field at harvesttime.

Each night after dinner, Ma Po-po threw herself before the open window and worshiped the moon; on moonless nights, she paid homage to the stars.

After finishing her prayers, the old woman escaped into the night, wearing a thin cotton garment—though shards of ice were beginning to float upon the ponds—only to return at cock's crow, with her long gray hair all ascatter.

A man was hired to trail her; her stooping figure was seen to enter temples and graveyards, there to become prostrate before unseen things.

Her family grew increasingly frightened of her. And because her own family was alarmed, one could imagine the degree of her neighbors' fright.

And again old men were heard to declare, "Demons will rise when the realm is in decline. Hear me out: when rulers fall, demons will fly." Upon hearing these words, folk fell into an appalled silence.

The nocturnal barking of the dogs jangled the nerves. The neighbors shivered under their quilts when they saw her moonshadow skimming across their papered windows. They shut their doors tight.

"Whatever's gobbling her up has got to be chucked out of her body and our home," her son said to his wife. He gathered the implements for a magic rite.

He filled a big rice bowl with water and encircled it with a ring of paper-cut men. A thick bundle of chopsticks was made to stand upright in the center of the bowl.

"Now I've nabbed that ol' demon in the prison of sticks," said the son.

He lit a match and set the ring of paper men on fire and, with one swift slice of the cleaver, sent the chopsticks scattering, clattering across the tabletop and onto the floor.

He dashed to the bedroom door and gave the threshold three whacks with the cleaver. He ran to the front door and *whack! whack! whack!* Out to the front gate and *whack! whack! whack!* chopping away at the thresholds with a vengeance.

Now that the demon had been evicted from their home, the front gate was slammed shut to prevent the devilish thing from reentering.

"We are now safe," the son pronounced, but it was only a thin statement of hope.

The ritual had no effect. Ma Po-po continued to mumble, "I'll fully become. . . . On the hundredth day, I'll have fully become. You all just wait and see: then, my power will be great. . . ."

Her nocturnal wanderings led her farther and farther from home. Her appetite continued to grow, yet the fingers she extended out from under the quilt as she cried, "Give us more grub!" remained yellow and thin.

"We can't afford to keep her, but neither can we get rid of her," said her son. "She's eaten up just about everything; soon she'll be gnawing upon the roof beams. Oh, what to do?" Having no other recourse, the family packed up their things and quietly, very quietly, disappeared from town.

"Can't have her running around loose like this, now that there's no one to keep an eye on her," the neighbors said.

A mob stormed into her home and tied her down to a bench with heavy ropes.

A sorcerer arrived with a magic horsetail fly whisk to shoo away evil; he invoked Daoist deities for protection; he used vermilion ink to draw occult diagrams upon three strips of yellow paper, one of which he pasted across the soles of her shoes, the second upon her bedroom door, and the third above the frame of the front door.

"The mystic power of the calligraphy will keep the demon from going out of the house," he said.

They left her tied to the bench, without food or water.

That night, the dogs yammered and yowled with great urgency, but no one dared to look outside. There was no moon to cast shadows, which made it all the more eerie, for they could smell her presence.

"I'm not afraid of any of you. Very soon, I'll have fully become . . . and then we shall see," said Ma Po-po when her neighbors found her the next day, seated under the shade of a somber old tree in her yard.

Again they bid the sorcerer to come perform his protective magic, but he had grown fearful of Ma Po-po's expanding power and feigned business at the opposite end of town.

Folk took the matter into their own hands. Once more, they hauled her to the bench and tied her down, but this time they threaded the two ends of the rope through the holes in a pair of granite millstones. It took eight men to lift the disks from the garden and set them resting upon their rims, flush against the bench, one to each side of the old woman's chest.

"If Blue Dragon, the good spirit of the millstones, cannot expel the demon . . . well, there won't be much else we can do," they said.

And this was as much as Baba had heard from Fourth Uncle the day the benevolent powers of Blue Dragon were invoked.

As shooting stars grazed the eastern sky the following evening, the townsfolk gathered as if summoned by a silent call. From the far corners of the city, they streamed to Temple Facing Temple, the section of town where Ma Po-po lived.

Baba and Fourth Uncle joined the hushed crowd that had gathered outside her gate.

Fourth Uncle wielded his treasured sword, which was believed to have the power to protect its master from harm. It was dubbed the Seven Star Sword, for indeed seven stars spangled the blade.

With a combined courage the size of a solitary pea, a cluster of men and boys inched into the darkened house. An icy shaft of moonlight thrust through a window and illuminated the hall; Baba could make out the still, supine form of the old woman upon the bench.

Had Blue Dragon squelched the evil spirit and the old woman along with it?

No one spoke; they were frozen like statuary. Each person was sure the others could hear the thumping of his heart, but each heard only his own.

"I ain't afraid of any of you," the old woman said all of a sudden in a small, thin voice. The men and boys gasped and snapped back like one taut spring.

"I'll have you all know that this is the ninety-ninth day."

Silence followed upon awful silence. When the men realized that she had not pounced, they were shamed by their display of nerves. A few slunk forward.

Fourth Uncle took the Seven Star Sword and lightly tapped the old woman upon her forehead with the flat of the cold blade. The stars gleamed blue in the moonlight. Ma Po-po did not let out a sound, but Baba could feel Fourth Uncle's arm trembling more violently than his own.

Crack! The smell of sulfur. A man had lit a match. "Open up your mouth, you old demon!" said he.

The woman obeyed like a child. The man tossed the flaming matchstick into her wide-open mouth.

"There, tell me what that is!" the man demanded.

Baba could hear the snap of the matchstick as the old woman bit down with her few remaining teeth.

"Well, come now—tell me what it is!"

"Ha ha! What it is? What it is? I'll tell you

what it is! It's the stem of a scrumptious pear." And with that, the old woman loudly smacked her lips.

As if on cue, the gathering of the brave—Baba and Fourth Uncle packed among them—stormed out of the hall in a tight knot like a many-legged beast.

When those who had hunched nervously just outside the garden gate heard the rapid *bata-bata-bata* of fleeing footsteps, they bolted in advance.

For a fortnight, no one dared enter the house.

Baba and Fourth Uncle did not make a return visit—ever—but they heard it rumored that when curiosity finally overcame Ma Po-po's neighbors, a few brave souls crept inside.

The hall was so still, it seemed one could hear the gnats straining in the cobwebs.

What had become of Ma Po-po? Surely she would have died from want of food and water.

When people's eyes adjusted to the gloom, they saw the ropes that had bound her coiled neatly on the floor. Where her feet had rested upon the bench, a pair of soiled embroidered shoes remained.

"The son must have come back and buried the body," someone said in a trembling voice. "She must be lying with the earthworms by now."

"Yes, yes, of course. This . . . this must be the reason for her disappearance," they said in unison, nodding at one another vigorously.

"But then tell me, where did the millstones go?" someone else said.

They searched the house and the yard, but the cumbersome stones were nowhere to be found.

The following year, in the autumn of 1945, the folk of Xinmin witnessed the fall of the Japanese puppet state of Manchukuo, and they were filled with joy, curiosity, and—not least—fear.

IN THE UNCERTAIN winter following the Japanese surrender, my father traveled to Zhoutuozi, in the countryside, to visit the family of his third uncle.

Early one morning, he was awakened by a pair of rude hands shaking his shoulders.

"Nephew! Number Four!" Baba heard. "Get up! I've seen an omen in the night!" When Baba wrested open his leaden lids, he saw the ecstatic figure of Third Uncle pacing the room. There was only a glimmer of dawn to the east.

"I've had a dream," his uncle said to him. "In this dream, a beauty descended from the sky in a swirl of silk and smoke, cradling a mahogany treasure chest in her arms. When she offered the chest to me, the lid sprung open, and thirty-six crimson bats fluttered out. Their shrill cries pierced the cocoon of my dream.

" 'Hmm . . . must be a sign—bats are symbolic of good fortune,' I said to myself, throwing off the quilt. 'The courtesan, Qingyun—Blue Cloud—has come to bring me good fortune.' "

Third Uncle abruptly stopped his pacing and stood before Baba.

"Nephew," he said, "I'll have you place a bet on this enchantress at the game of *huahui* today. I'll wager a big sum at the lottery—bigger than they've ever seen. Scare them a little, those men of the 'black society.' And if I win—ah! that'll be even better; I'll break their bank."

Third Uncle was not a gambler, but this dashing, impressive gesture he could not resist; being the newly appointed magistrate of Zhoutuo County, he wanted to make his power keenly felt.

"With the Japanese gone and the Chinese government just staggering to its feet," he continued on, as if talking to himself, "those hoodlums running the lottery are taking mighty great liberties in this vacuum. Their swaggering behavior has gotten way out of hand."

Third Uncle sat down at the table. "Qingyun," he wrote on a scrap of red paper, which he folded into a tight little square and then placed inside the metal case of a spent cartridge.

Next, he inserted a thin strip of paper. Upon the length that extended out of the case was written the extravagant sum "One hundred yuan," followed by his own name: "Yang the Incorruptible." He hammered shut the opening, which caused the strip to be clamped securely in place.

Once this was accomplished, he handed Baba the sealed cartridge, along with a roll of money.

"Go quickly to where they are holding the lottery this morning—if I'm not wrong, it's at the House of Li on this day," he said.

Upon arrival in Manchuria, back in 1931, the Japanese had banned the big business of gambling, clamping down on the "black societies" that ran them; they knew the influential underworld would be primed to plot their overthrow. (Small, private games like *paijiu*—dominoes—and mah-jongg were left alone.) But now that they were gone, the gambling establishments again mushroomed; and especially now, in these economically unstable times, a great many folk could be expected to patronize the lotteries, hanging their hopes on making a quick fortune.

A few cool stars still dangled in the east as Baba clambered onto the back of a little donkey. "Trrr, trrr," he cried to urge the beast on, but the animal stumbled and knelt in the furrows hidden in the snow; Baba would find himself sliding headfirst down the neck of the beast.

As a fresh blanket of white had erased all traces of the road, Baba steered the donkey toward a distant grove of leafless poplars, above which thin threads of smoke curled, telling of dwellings.

Horse-drawn carts and wagons lined the road that led up to the House of Li; many had come from neighboring villages to place their bets. Many more were arriving on foot. Over two hundred could be expected on this day, for it was just before the Lunar New Year—a time of rest when folk gathered to crack melon seeds, to exchange stories, and to gossip.

Baba tied his donkey to a fence post and

walked up to the house, with its gently rounded roof—the overall shape like a thick loaf of bread, the design typical of Manchuria. He walked past two husky peasants with rifles, standing guard at the front door. The Japanese had also banned firearms, but now the guns had been dug out of buried caches.

Once he was through the entrance, a rush of warm air enveloped his body; he felt his lips tingle as they began to thaw; he had entered the kitchen, with its four big stoves. Laughter, chatter, and tobacco smoke issued from a door. Baba entered the left wing of the house. The screen partitions separating the adjoining series of rooms had been removed, and he now found himself in a vast rectangular hall.

It was filled with villagers, bundled in their puffy quilted jackets, bobbing their heads and gesturing with their hands in animated talk. There were men with tea-stained teeth; gaffers without teeth; matrons smoking long-stemmed pipes; peasant girls with chapped red cheeks, who came to stake their meager earnings from gleaning soybeans the previous summer. A good number of these crusty, weathered faces belonged to professional runners—men who relayed bets for a percentage of the winnings.

Folk sat along the length of the north and south walls, upon two kang, nearly every available square inch of whose space had been taken. Others sat upon the rows of benches set on the floor between the kang.

The game of *huahui* reached every layer of rural society: it had its fingers in the silk-lined pockets of the rich as well as in the pockets of the poor filled with only a few coppers; the men who ran the *huahui* reaped money the way farmers harvested peanuts: a tug on the vine brought in all the pods, big and small, growing on interconnected fibers underground.

It was Baba's turn to register Third Uncle's bet.

As he approached the short table set up on the northern kang, he heard a man in conversation refer to him: "This young'un in front is the grandson of the big landlord and the nephew of the magistrate, just come from the city."

It was the beginning of winter break for seventeen-year-old Baba, in his first year at the Shenyang Polytechnic; he had many joyous days ahead of him to explore the countryside. He was feeling buoyant, excited to be among the villagers, loving nothing more than to listen to ghost stories in dialect on long evenings.

A bespectacled man with a thin, brittle face sat behind the table and registered the names of the gamblers and the amounts they were betting. His heavy glasses pinched his nose as he pawed through the pages of a ledger. This was Old Li, the overseer.

He resembles some sort of blind, snouted animal, rooting around in the undergrowth, thought Baba.

To the man's left were two rather well-fed, oily-skinned men, who licked their thumbs to facilitate the counting of the stacks of paper money set before them. The cackle of coins, the crisp *click-clack*s of the abacus, provided music so mesmerizing, they barely glanced up from their work. A scattering of cartridges, similar to the one in Baba's hand, lay on the crowded table, along with simpler affairs: tightly folded squares of paper that also enclosed bets, with the name of the gambler and the amount staked written on the outside.

When Baba placed Third Uncle's sealed cartridge on the table and gently set the thick wad of money next to it, Old Li peered up at him; his spectacles magnified the astonishment in his eyes, but he quickly tried to mask his response. He smiled, revealing his lower teeth.

Baba jostled for a perch on the kang, a couple of feet away from the table, and settled down to watch the proceedings.

Behind the three men rested the altar to the God of Prosperity. With his placid, Buddha eyes, the god gazed down upon the congregation as if he were able to pierce the facades and see through to all the hearts. Old Li lit the incense and candles at the altar; he prayed for the safekeeping of the house.

This was how the game of *huahui* was played:

From among thirty-six names—figures from history, legends, and lore—three were to be selected according to the whims and intuitions of the hosts. Upon the announcement of each of the three names, the reaction of the crowd was carefully studied: excitement and agitation easily betrayed the simple countryfolk. Some fiddled with their pipes, some jiggled their knees; most tried in vain to look unflustered. But under the aggressive scrutiny of the "eyes"—the dozen or so village ne'er-do-wells hired to watch for telltale signs of inner disquiet, whose shadowy figures glided silently among the crowd like wraiths—all nervous displays were noted and whispered as information into the ears of Old Li and his two sidekicks.

The three chosen names were to be written in ink on red paper and posted next to the altar.

From these three names, one final name would be selected—the one that seemed to have created a minimal stir in the crowd. At the end of the day, those who had placed their money on this one particular figure would go home fat and happy, with thirty-six times the amount of money they had come to stake.

Therefore, with one hundred yuan wagered by Third Uncle, the possibility of losing the vast sum of thirty-six hundred yuan loomed darkly over the heads of the three who ran the game; the "eyes" were admonished to keep close watch over Baba.

Boom! Boom! Boom! The papered windows and the rafters shuddered. Three shots had been fired at the air by the guards outside, stunning the congregation into silence. The sudden blasts were said to be good for expelling demons, but the real purpose was to intimidate the gathering—to strain the nerves, all the better for seeing each minute twitch, hearing every subdued hum. Like the switching off of an electric light, the clamorous hall was suddenly hushed; a heavy, breathing quiet fell, and not one soul spoke; the smokers continued to draw instinctively on their pipes. No more bets could now be placed.

"Number one!" cried Old Li. "Qingyun the Seductress!"

The men behind the table watched Baba. A sudden draft made the candles at the altar flicker and the flames go tall. Little could be read from Baba's smooth, whiskerless young face.

For a long interval, the men who ran the games surveyed the sea of faces, sniffed for fear, extended their antennae for muffled vibrations. Their eyes probed the far corners, for they knew that those who sat farthest from the table were the timid ones, whose emotions were the most easily revealed.

"Number two! Wu Song the Tiger Slayer!" declared Old Li, his face bloodless and severe.

Baba sat on the kang, admiring the New Year prints. "How bright and friendly they are," he said to himself. "When I get a chance, I'd like to paint something in those colors."

He felt no tension; after all, it wasn't his money wagered.

Again the protracted scrutiny. In the silence, one could very well have heard a grain of rice skitter across the floor. It was twice eternity for those who had placed their bets on the Tiger Slayer.

"Number three! Monkey King the Trickster!"

Baba's eyes now rested on the whimsical paper cuts pasted on the windows. An entire menagerie of farm animals—dogs, geese, chickens, donkeys, sows, and piglets—danced in noisy profusion across the sill; yes, there was even a baby cow, riding pickaback on the papa cow.

A man gnawed on his knuckles. Another drew with increasing frequency on his pipe, cloaking himself in smoke.

Huddled together, their foreheads almost touching, Old Li and his two cohorts whispered, compared notes, consulted one another: "Well, how's it look; which of the three will it be?"

A person entering the hall at that moment would have felt the vibration of a heavy, low sound, suppressed. Much was at stake.

Men and women went to great lengths to choose the one figure that augured wealth.

Some villagers wrapped thirty-six dumplings, each containing one of the thirty-six names. With a stolen—not borrowed—rice ladle belonging to a widow (innumerable rice ladles disappeared from the home of Baba's widowed fifth aunt during her lifetime), the first dumpling to float to the surface of the boiling pot of water was scooped out and its secret probed.

There were other methods: those with a taste for the macabre entered graveyards under the mantle of night and threw thirty-six scraps of paper, each piece written with a different name, into one of the holes dug by nesting foxes in burial mounds. Taking a wooden rake, they extracted a single scrap that would reveal the auspicious name.

The men who ran the games performed their own elaborate ceremonies in terrible secrecy to counter the prayers and magic of the villagers, but sometimes, in the more unscrupulous gambling houses, deception of a thespian nature was resorted to in order to influence the outcome.

Before an audience gathered at the *huahui,* the overseer would give one of his assistants a tongue-lashing: "I told you last time, you stupid squash, never call the Monkey King! It is bad luck for us!" A slap to the noggin of the "stupid squash" would emphasize his point.

At the next gathering, no one would think to bet a single copper on the Monkey King; and of course, the Monkey King would be ultimately selected.

After what seemed like hours, the hushed talk of the three fellows at the table finally ceased, and Old Li faced the crowd.

The sweet fragrance of incense seemed unusually heavy. A magpie shrieked, and children called far away. The gathering breathed as one being, though each man's heart was locked in his own desires.

"Qiiingyuuuun the Enchantress!" called Old Li, dragging out the vowels. *Crack!* He slammed a block of wood down upon the table to seal the decision.

Tension washed away. Sighs and exclamations rent the air as the hall reverted to its original hubbub and din.

Baba felt joy and amusement: he had helped Third Uncle win thirty-six hundred yuan—an astronomical sum to countryfolk. He remained seated and continued to watch the movements in the hall.

Unfolding themselves from the kang and the benches, the villagers stretched and dusted off their clothes. They shook their heads, vowing to go home rich the next time. "I'll have my day yet!" a man was heard to say.

A knot of jabbering, excited folk crowded around the table to claim their winnings.

"I'm going to get myself a couple of yards of that flower print I've been wanting," a girl said, and she blushed as bright as a peony.

"What a wonderful Spring Festival this will be—more meat in the dumplings instead of so much cabbage," an old man said. "Maybe I'll buy the wife a jade mouthpiece for her pipe."

"No, I'm not gonna be buying trinkets," said another. "Going to get a gun, now that I can afford one; can't afford not to have one, now with strange rumblings in the countryside and, as I've heard it, way up north, too. I tell you, I'm gettin' some real nasty feelings in my bones about

things to come. . . . Don't know what to expect, but I don't expect much good."

When the crowd around the table thinned out, Baba quietly approached. Old Li shifted uncomfortably. The two others at the table looked up from their ledgers.

"Well, young sir, how did the magistrate do?" wheezed Old Li.

"*Beng le*—the bullet has burst," Baba replied.

The rattle of the abacus abated. For a long astonished moment, no one stirred. Only the fitful shadows cast by the candles shifted across the altar; the God of Prosperity seemed to wink.

Old Li swallowed hard. *"B-b-beng le?"* he stammered. He pried open the cartridge casing that Third Uncle had so carefully sealed, and extracted the square of red paper within.

"Qingyun," he read, once his shaking hands had managed to unfold it. There was no mistaking what was written.

A low moan was heard out of him, such as was never before heard in the hall. The other two fellows stared at Baba mutely, their faces tight and pallid.

Someone nearby said in a loud voice: "This proves the adage: 'City kids and country dogs are too wily to outwit.' "

Old Li unbuttoned the collar of his silk jacket and peered at Baba over his fogged spectacles. Once he had regained his voice, he said, "You'd best be getting on home; there's no use in waiting round today." His voice was soft yet disquieting. "You can well understand we don't have that kind of money here. Please tell the magistrate I'll be calling on him first thing tomorrow morning."

Baba emerged from the smoke-filled house. The sun was high in the cobalt sky, and the icicles under the eaves were melting. He breathed deeply. Men and women milling outside gazed at him with admiration.

"Now, that's one I wouldn't mind for a son-in-law," a woman said. "Such a large sum at stake, and that young'un just sat there right under their noses and held a straight face." The villagers shook their heads and clicked their tongues and muttered, "City kids . . . too wily, too wily."

Baba trotted home on the little donkey. The smooth fields of snow were now cupped by the sun.

On most days, Third Uncle, the magistrate, a pistol tucked under his waistcoat, would have been making his daily rounds upon his white horse, flanked by two rifle-bearing bodyguards on black mules. But today Baba found him pacing about in his study with high energy. The gleam in his eyes accompanied the pride and ambition expressed in his voice.

"Yes, yes, you needn't tell me," he said, with a brusque wave of his thick hands at Baba. "The good news has preceded you; everyone has heard of my victory over those good-for-nothings. I knew this would be a very satisfactory day. I shall enjoy seeing them with their tails between their legs." A smile played on his ruddy, round face.

The following morning, just after breakfast,

Old Li arrived with two horse-drawn wagons filled to mounding peaks with black beans, the value of which was far less than the thirty-six hundred yuan that Third Uncle had won; but it was the gesture that mattered—a gesture symbolic of compliance; an acknowledgment of defeat.

Old Li waited for Third Uncle outside the gate, his hands fidgeting with his hat, his shoulders slightly hunched.

With long, generous strides, Third Uncle approached him. He patted the man on the back and said:

"Yes, yes, Old Li, this will do. This will do nicely."

Third Uncle was not interested in the money; he was solely concerned with flexing his muscles. So preoccupied was he by the sense of his own power, he did not see the hatred that simmered in the other man's eyes.

Old Li bowed and smiled and bowed, but after Third Uncle had turned his back to go, Baba heard the man say, in a small voice that chilled him: "Just you wait and see, Your Honor . . . he who gambles long enough always loses."

Years later, under the banner of men who claimed to be the voice of the people, Old Li led the peasants to ransack Third Uncle's home and grain storage; Third Uncle lost three toes on his right foot as he fled the rabble in the snow and ice. Later, in a labor camp, he even lost his life.

But these events, looming in the future, neither my father, his third uncle, Old Li—nor anyone else, for that matter—could possibly have guessed, in that dubious winter following the Japanese defeat.

"HAI, NUMBER FOUR," Uncle Zhao, a hired hand, said with a sigh to my father. "The world is changing fast, too fast. Much of it I don't understand . . . but I know it's time for me to make some changes too."

In winter of 1945–46, following the Japanese defeat, many were thinking to do just that.

Uncle Zhao had been with the House of Yang for over thirteen years now. His appearance in the autumn of 1932, when Baba was only three, had been courtesy of the Japanese, newly arrived in 1931.

The notorious "Skinner" and his underlings hunted bandits relentlessly for their new masters, the Japanese. The Japanese waged fierce campaigns to eradicate the marauding redbeards in the countryside.

When Skinner and his men caught their prey, they flayed them alive and hung their skins from a tree by the roadside, to dry like laundry.

Zhao, a clumsy redbeard from the neighborhood of Shantuozi, tumbled off his horse as Skinner and his men gave chase; he was scooped up from the dust like a stunned rabbit.

"I was abducted by the bandits," he said to his captors (his mind, you see, was not so clumsy).

"You certainly do not look the part of a redbeard," Skinner said, studying the man's unimpressive features. He decided not to dull his knife that day on Zhao's hide. Instead he tossed the man into the Xinmin County prison.

News of Zhao's plight reached his sister. She journeyed from Shantuozi to Xinmin. There, she pleaded with the Patriarch of the House of Yang to intervene on her brother's behalf; she believed the influential old gentleman, born and raised in Shantuozi, would speak up for one sprung from the same soil.

Zhao was released when the Patriarch appeared before the authorities; he guaranteed the man's future good behavior. Having no place to go, Zhao the ex-bandit asked to stay on at the

House of Yang. He became the caretaker of the North and South Gardens.

It was not until my father returned to Manchuria from Beiping, at the age of eleven, that he would come to know "Uncle Zhao."

Solid and strong, stolid but amiable, he was a man of few words. Baba never heard the man laugh from the belly; he only saw an occasional smile seep into the corners of his mouth.

"Big Uncle Zhao, I'm hungry," was Baba's customary cry to the man when he returned home from school. "Can you help me find an eggplant to eat?" Uncle Zhao would not allow the children to damage the bulbs with their fingernails as they tested the shiny green Manchurian eggplants for ripeness; he knew the sweetest ones by sight.

Nor would he allow Old Lady Lu to let her chickens and ducks run loose; yet he patiently picked jars of cabbage worms for her greedy flocks to eat.

"It's time for dinner, Uncle Zhao!" Baba often hollered to the figure bent over the cabbages; otherwise the man would have lingered in the garden long after dusk.

Baba was a frequent visitor to the room next to the mill where Uncle Zhao and another hired hand, named Yu, lived. This sanctuary, smelling of corn flour and hay, was where he often hid from grown-ups who threatened beatings—for raising doves; for running on the roof.

Here, he would try on Uncle Zhao's big *wula* shoes, so called because the leather shoes were filled with special *wula* grass, which grew only on the Manchurian plains; it kept one's feet especially warm and dry in the winter.

"Aiya, Number Four," said Uncle Zhao to Baba, shaking his head in mock exasperation. "Have you been foolin' with my pair of *wula* again? Now you make me have to repad them to get them to fit right."

It was a special treat for Baba if Uncle Zhao, in a rare talkative mood, spoke of his past.

"We poor boys always dreamed of pulling our feet out of the mud, out of the soil. Many of us joined the redbeards—I joined up at eighteen—thinking it was a sure way to leave behind our hard life tied to the land. Maybe we believed too much in the warriors of legends and history—beggars who became emperors," said the man as he sat cross-legged on the kang, his strong hands doing the delicate mending of the reed mats upon which he slept.

"All I knew as an orphan was that I wanted to wear polished riding boots and carry a sword someday as a big man in the military. And joining the redbeards, I thought, would give me such a chance."

"Why's that?" Baba asked, plumping himself down on the heated kang to sit wedged between Uncle Zhao and Yu, the roommate.

"Well, if a bandit group grew big enough and came to control a large enough territory, the government honored them by inducting them to form a new division of the army.

"But after ten years with the redbeards, I was no closer to my dream; our small group was still running around raiding hamlets like yellow weasels. If we had grown powerful enough, the people would've been bringing us grain and treasures on their own, just as they make offerings to temple gods.

"And as for me, after ten years, I hadn't risen above the position of groom and lookout, always eating last at the banquets. Too awkward, I guess . . . just couldn't get the knack of it . . . just couldn't stay on my horse."

"Lao Zhao—Old Zhao," said Yu, scratching his scalp and peering at his friend from under droopy eyelids, "it wasn't your fault. Life is beyond our control. It's all a matter of timing—a matter of luck, you know. What's that saying . . . ? Oh, yes: 'Only when Heaven, Earth, and fellowman smile upon the hour can success be had.' Got to have all three elements working for you at the same time."

Uncle Zhao sighed and wagged his large head. Baba left him to his reveries.

When wagons fitted with inflated rubber tires became popular in Manchuria, the Patriarch, eager to keep up with the times, replaced the family's old wagons, with their steel-rimmed wooden wheels. The faster new wagons were used to haul wheat and sorghum from the countryside to the Patriarch's granaries in Xinmin City.

He recruited Uncle Zhao as the driver and relieved him of the more strenuous work in the gardens, for he had seen silver strands appearing at the man's temples.

"A fellow should be thinking about padding his nest for old age, Lao Zhao," said the Patriarch, standing with his hands clasped behind his back. The old gentleman's eyes were fierce to behold, but those who worked for him knew his heart to be as soft as bean curd.

"You are welcome to use the horse and wagon to earn some extra money—hauling goods for others," he said. "Whatever you make on the side is entirely yours to keep."

Uncle Zhao was pleased with the new arrangement, and he continued on at the House of Yang as the family wagoner.

Baba loved to go for rides. Proud Uncle Zhao swung the whip high in the air, making it sing *so-so-so-so-so* in its revolutions; like a young buck, the middle-aged man mischievously raced the fashionable, sleek new wagon past the weary old models plodding along on the road, the wagoners looking on with tight-lipped envy.

One winter, several years down the line, Uncle Zhao was hired by a fruit vendor in Xinmin. He ventured out alone. The road was frozen hard; on an especially bad section, the wagon went into a skid and overturned, smashing the crates and spilling the fruit.

"Aiya, my friend. We are certainly short on luck today," he said as he patted the mare on the neck. The horse shook her head as if she understood his distress. (She had a white coat dappled with spots of rusty red, patterned just like the oranges now dotting the snow. He had never once used the whip on her but cracked it high in the air.)

The Patriarch did not wish Uncle Zhao to pay for the damage; he purchased the entire wagonload from the fruit vendor.

"They are only slightly blemished; we will be needing oranges for the New Year celebrations anyway," Baba heard the Patriarch say.

Uncle Zhao thanked him, but his spirit had been bruised more severely than the fruits.

Good fortune rarely arrives in pairs; misfortune never arrives alone: so goes the saying.

The following week, as Uncle Zhao drove to market with Baba's ever-exuberant second brother, a tottering old peasant, balancing two baskets of purple radishes upon a shoulder pole, rammed one end of the pole against the head of the mare as he tried to cross the street. The startled horse galloped off, throwing Uncle Zhao—who had never been known for his agility—off his perch on the sideboard and onto the ice. The mare tore off in a fury, with Second Brother in the back of the wagon, enjoying what promised to be a most invigorating ride.

Uncle Zhao pulled himself up off the snow and ice and padded after the animal, but his loose-fitting *wula* shoes proved unsuitable for the chase, and he gave it up after sustaining two spectacular spills.

The horse blazed across town, all the way to the neighborhood of "Granddaddy Temple"—built in honor of Guangong, the God of War. There she was reined in by a passerby.

It was no fault of Uncle Zhao's that the old peasant with the radishes had fallen, that he lay thrashing and moaning on the ground. He was soon hustled off to the hospital.

Word got around town that the peasant had been crushed to death by the wagon owned by wealthy Yang Laojun, the Patriarch at the House of Yang. "And not only that," folk said. "The driver was also dragged under the wheels like the radishes—hai, a most horrible sight. . . . But more horrible yet was the coarse-looking lass with big, broad shoulders seated in the back of the wagon. She was laughing hysterically as the wagon went flying off."

The police apprehended Uncle Zhao for manslaughter and threw him in jail. The following morning, the Patriarch arrived to clear up the situation and take the poor man home.

Meanwhile, the old peasant, who in reality

had sustained only a few bruises, had found the comfort of the hospital more to his liking than his own mud hut and refused to go home.

"My 'lantern hanger' pains me," he bleated, baring his pink gums. Baba and the other visitors from the House of Yang could not figure out just where his "lantern hanger" was on his person, but they knew for certain that the old codger had no intention of vacating the hospital bed—at least not until the wealthy Patriarch imparted some of his wealth to him. Only after the peasant had been given two hundred yuan did he take his "lantern hanger" home with him to the village.

Following upon the latest mishap, Uncle Zhao became a man of even fewer words and had no more stories of his bandit days to tell. "I have become the Patriarch's burden" were the only words out of him.

"Put it behind you, Lao Zhao. It wasn't your fault. No one blames you," said the Patriarch. "We must celebrate the Spring Festival as always."

But Uncle Zhao's self-recriminations were piling high upon his soul like snow straining the roof. Baba watched him sit in his room, puffing on his long pipe, repairing the harnesses, fixing the bridles, fastening new lashes on the tips of the whips; he ventured out on the wagon only when the family had specific holiday errands for him to run.

Each year on New Year's Eve, Uncle Zhao treated the younger children to a wagon ride through the snow to welcome the God of Prosperity; it had never bothered him to change out of his holiday best—his long blue gown—and into his work clothes in order to play chauffeur to the children.

"The God of Prosperity is back! The God has returned!" the children screamed as firecrackers snapped and Uncle Zhao cracked his long whip in the midnight sky.

This year, however, the children were reluctant to disturb him.

"Uncle Zhao, what are you thinking about?" Baba asked as he tiptoed into the man's room.

At seventeen, he was much too old for wagon rides but was still an inveterate visitor to the room next to the mill. The walls were decorated with bright New Year prints, many of which depicted fat babies embracing melons or riding upon huge carp: wishes for abundance and many offspring.

"Hai, Number Four," Uncle Zhao said with a sigh, and he gazed upon the wall posters. "Let me fill my pipe, and then I'll tell you what's been on my mind. . . . The Japanese have gone now . . . since autumn. The world is changing fast, too fast. Much of it I don't understand . . . but I know it's time for me to make some changes too.

"I want to return home to Shantuozi. There, I've an old sister; we'll be good company for each other. I want to be the master of my own plot of land—that's what I want most of all. And maybe I might find myself a wife. Have a go at another dream. . . ." His impassive expression had gradually given way to one of longing. "Maybe I'll get the timing right—have some luck on my side this time, eh?"

Upon hearing Uncle Zhao's decision, the Patriarch was pleased. He gave the man ten mu of land in Shantuozi and asked him to choose any horse from the stable.

Uncle Zhao, naturally, picked his favorite: the faithful dappled mare—the silent witness to her master's many spills upon the winter roads. She was incredibly strong; hunching her back, she was capable of hauling the loaded wagon up the sharp inclines at railroad crossings and out of the spring mire hidden to the eye by a thin crust of sunbaked earth. Most horses would have been helpless in these situations.

One ensuing spring morning when the smooth branches of the willows had yet to bud with fuzzy silver-green "willow dogs," the family stood in the yard to say good-bye.

They watched Uncle Zhao tie his scant belongings to the saddle. The man, now even clumsier with age, made two labored attempts before he was able to hoist himself onto the mare and then slowly ride out the South Gate.

"Well, let's hope he doesn't tumble off his

horse this time around," Baba heard Yu, standing next to him, quip. But Baba saw that Yu was not laughing: two dark blotches stained his cotton-padded jacket; perhaps one tear was for Uncle Zhao, the other for himself.

"Let's hope he'll stay upright. Perhaps he'll do well in his new life as a landowner," Yu continued.

But Baba and Yu both knew times were changing, and no one could be certain of anything. Not of Heaven, not of Earth, not of fellowman.

YU, WHOM EVERYONE in the family called "Uncle Yu," had come to the House of Yang in the winter of 1940, soon after my father's return to Manchuria.

The hired hand worked the North and South Gardens in the summer, but his greatest importance to the family was in the winter, when he was charged with the duty of breaking the ice that formed over the old well.

In wintertime, it became difficult and dangerous for the women to bring up water, for it sloshed out of the bucket and froze around the mouth of the well, causing the ice to ring higher with each successive draw; those who climbed the steep, slippery slope to reach the water were in danger of falling down into the belly of the well. Uncle Yu would swing a pickax to break the cone of ice.

It was easy for folk to see that he was of peasant stock: a flat face known to northerners as *da bing zi lian*—big pancake face; sleepy eyes, long and narrow, which never registered astonishment, even when it was deeply felt; his upper lip curled to reveal big front teeth, flecked with brown; when he walked, his long arms dangled simian-like out in front of him.

Baba and his cousins secretly referred to the man as "Baldy Gone Bad," the reason being that when he scratched—whether his shiny shaved pate, behind his ears, or his elbows and knees—he rained tiny white shards of skin.

On many a winter night, Uncle Yu sat cross-legged upon the kang, patching and repatching a hand-me-down pair of *wula* shoes, discarded years ago by Uncle Zhao. Uncle Yu laughed to himself, the noise sounding like small bursts of air escaping out of a rubber tire. When Baba asked him what tickled him so, he replied:

"I've poked these tired old winter shoes so many times with a needle, if it was a live critter it would cry 'Ji! Ji! Ji!' in displeasure." His long, narrow eyes stretched even longer in mirth.

The few cherished items he owned, he placed in a small cloth satchel: a pair of new cotton shoes; a glossy silk skullcap, topped with a red pompon; and a floor-length blue gown, which was always neatly folded.

At noon on the last day of the year, when the Spring Festival celebrations began, Uncle Yu would emerge like a blushing bride in his precious attire, which smelled musty from long storage.

"Happy—happy New Year, Elder Sister," he would stammer to Nainai as he stared down at his shoes.

After the fifth of the month, when Spring Festival came to an end, his things were carefully returned to the satchel, to wait out the seasons of toil.

Baba and the other children knew Uncle Yu to be good-natured. When they asked him to sing them a song, without hesitation the grown-up hopped birdlike and waved his arms, all the while warbling a fragment of a ditty:

"Nine goblins and eighteen caves, in every cave lives a goblin."

"More, please, Uncle Yu!" clamored the children.

The man would shrug his shoulders and say: "Oh, but I haven't any more." He had sung his entire repertoire.

But Uncle Yu had a way of making it up to the young ones for his lack of songs: in late spring, when flocks of colorful birds came up from the south, he helped the children ensnare them without harming a feather. He was a skillful trapper.

One year, when weasels were wreaking havoc in the chicken coop, the family enlisted Uncle Yu's help to catch the varmints.

He set his traps and waited. And waited. Not one weasel consented to be ensnared. But unwittingly, he himself came to be the prey.

As he sat upon the kang one day, his body began to tremble.

When asked what ailed him, he replied in a curious accent and intonation common to folk from the province of Shandong to the south, but quite foreign to his everyday talk:

"I am the spirit of the Yellow Weasel. I've come to avenge myself upon the rascal Yu, who wishes to do me harm."

"Spirit, where do you live?" folk asked.

"In the front, in the back, to the left and to the right." No one had ever seen Uncle Yu's sleepy eyes opened so wide.

Baba's father was called upon to expel the demon from the man's body. Yeye grabbed hold of Uncle Yu and made him sit on the threshold of the front door, facing inward; he then force-fed him a hard-boiled egg upon which was written magic words in vermilion ink. In this manner the spirit was chased out of the man's body and made to return to its hole.

As spring lapsed into summer, Uncle Yu began tending the gardens and did odd jobs on the grounds of the House of Yang; there really was very little for him to do during warm weather.

No one knew who had put the idea into his head, but one day in the summer of 1942, when Baba was thirteen, Uncle Yu announced that he had hired himself out as a laborer.

Manchuria was still under Japanese rule, and each assigned unit of ten families was forced to offer up one male laborer for a period of six months. Manpower was in short supply in the sparsely populated northeast as it was, and the families could not spare a single soul; in most cases, they pooled their money and bought the sweat and sinew of a poor man to take the place of one of their own.

No one knew how much Uncle Yu had sold himself for.

On the day of his departure, he handed Nainai his satchel for safekeeping. "Elder Sister," he said, "I'll be back by the end of fall."

When the autumn winds sent the leaves sighing and crashing onto the ground, Uncle Yu had not returned; when the snow was waist deep and ice crowned the well, the man was still absent; when the New Year was bruited with firecrackers, he was not to be seen, demure and sheepish in his holiday best; spring arrived and with it the flocks of birds, yet he had not returned to help the children set their traps. Where is Uncle Yu? everyone wondered.

On a summer day, when cool weather was but an alluring memory, Baba sat upon the kang, eating the midday meal with the family. Through the north window, whence came a breeze to provide gentle remedy, Baba saw a man push open the North Garden gate and saunter in, swinging his long simian arms.

"That sure looks like Uncle Yu," Baba said.

"It is Uncle Yu!" the rest of the children cried in unison. They threw down their chopsticks and stuck their heads out the window.

The man smiled his familiar toothy grin, revealing those flecks of brown.

The cheering children ran out, grabbed him by the hands, dragged him inside, and sat him down on the kang.

"Boys, run out and buy some fried pancakes, while I scramble up some eggs with chives," said Nainai. "We must celebrate this happy day."

And when all had finally settled down to eat, Uncle Yu began his story:

"In the center of Xinmin, we had assembled. From there we were taken to Shenyang. The truck bounced a lot, but we were fairly comfortable.

"In Shenyang, all us workers from this entire Liaoning Province were gathered together. Little did we expect the nightmare that would follow—didn't expect that we would lose our freedom. . . ." Uncle Yu picked at the food in his bowl, seeming unable to swallow.

"We were prodded onto airless boxcars like oxen. Once the big steel doors clanged shut, there was no way to get out. We couldn't see outside except by climbing the walls to peek between the slats just below the ceiling.

"Aiya, and in no time the smell, oh, the stink of so many bodies crammed together—the human stink and waste . . . I could barely breathe.

"I lost count of the days. We jogged north—sidetracked a lot of times while southbound trains rumbled past.

"When we finally got to Harbin—way up in the north part, in the direction of Russia—we were hauled by trucks to a wild, lonely place. Didn't know where we were.

"Nor did we know what the Japanese had

us constructing out there in the middle of no-where; we only knew it was something big.

"Yah, very big. Thousands of us sweated behind the barbed-wire enclosure. We dug and hauled soil all day long. But the only things we were given to eat were cold boiled potatoes and watery sorghum porridge.

"I had agreed to work for half a year, but after that amount of time had gone by, the Japanese wouldn't let me go. . . .

"The winter was the coldest, most terrible, I'd ever known—or ever wish to know again.

"Many died. When men got sick, they were carried to a fenced-off area. And only when I got sick myself did I really get a taste of how bad it could be. No one cared for us.

"I lay burning up in a fever for days. They didn't think I'd make it, so they hauled me outside the barbed wire on a plank. They carried me for a great, long distance, to a place where the dead were buried. It was spring already, and the grass had grown tall."

"The Chinese workers saw that I was still breathing; they must have felt pity and didn't throw dirt over me . . . hhhai."

Uncle Yu sat stock-still, hanging his head, letting the sigh drain out of him. Baba saw the rims of his eyes redden. No one dared break the silence; only the cooing of the doves upon the rooftop could be heard. The pancakes, the fragrant scrambled eggs with chives, sat upon the table, growing cold. Then the man mopped his face with his black, callused hands and continued:

"Someone gave me two rice sacks to lie on. *Whoosh-whoosh,* the wind would blow all night long through the grass.

"Sometimes, as the workers came out with more corpses, they nudged me with their toes to see if I was still alive. A kind soul left me a couple of raw potatoes.

"How many days I lay on that knoll, I can't figure now, but one night I came out of the fever. My body felt much lighter. I ate the potatoes, and after a bit I felt stronger. I crawled on my hands and knees through the grass, away from the burial place.

"At daybreak, I saw a village in the distance. I continued that awful crawl and finally reached a cornfield. The unripened corn tasted sweet and eased my thirst some. When I regained a bit more strength, I inched on.

"By noon, I had made it to the boundary between a cornfield and a field of sorghum, and there I saw three men at their noonday meal. They also saw me. They came after me.

"I was afraid they'd return me to the slave camp, so I tried to hide.

" 'Where're you from?' one man said when they grabbed hold of me. Well, they could see well enough from my condition where I'd come from.

"Then those good men gave me water and sweet bean cakes to eat. Ai, let me tell you, nothing had ever tasted so good! They told me the region was called Sankeshu—Triple Tree. And at dusk they propped me up and took me back to their village. I realized then that Heaven didn't intend for me to die just yet."

Uncle Yu shook his head. His eyes smiled just a little. He tore off a chunk of pancake and slowly chewed.

"I told them I knew how to work the land—knew how to drive wagons. I stayed in that village and helped them through the spring.

"They were good to me; they paid me for my work. They asked me to stay on, for there were even fewer men way up north—they needed all the help they could get. But I was homesick. . . .

"The folk there wrote down the directions for getting back here to Xinmin. I showed that piece of paper at the train stations, and people pointed out the way."

"Uncle Yu, how much did the ten families pay you to work for the Japanese?" Baba asked.

Uncle Yu smiled big.

"Elder Sister," he said to Nainai. "Can you get me my satchel?" When Nainai returned with the bag, the man pulled out one of his holiday shoes and fished in its recesses.

One by one, out came his tobacco, tinderbox, and pipe, and finally, from the toe of the shoe, he pulled out a square of paper. He ironed out its many neat folds and, like a magician, displayed a rare one-hundred-yuan note.

It was the largest currency in circulation in Japanese-controlled Manchukuo. Folk called it the "sheep bill," because pictured on one side was a flock of woolly sheep.

Uncle Yu beamed with pride and happiness as he silently studied the money—front and back. He held it up to the light. He gazed at it for a long while. When finally satisfied—knowing that after all those dark months it was now fully his—he refolded the money and placed it back inside the toe of his shoe. He retained his tobacco and pipe, however, for now that he was safely home, he could enjoy a good smoke again.

Nainai remained the keeper of the little cloth satchel, but now that she knew what it contained, she hid it deeper inside the wardrobe.

"Uncle Yu," folk said in the first month of 1944, "it's nearly Lunar New Year after all; why not buy something special with that sheep bill of yours? Surely you deserve to spend some money on yourself."

Uncle Yu grinned and shook his head. He continued to patch his hand-me-down *wula* shoes.

In the year that followed, he worked the garden in the summer as usual and removed the ice growing around the mouth of the well in the winter.

In the summer of 1945, Manchukuo was no more. The Japanese had been defeated.

"Uncle Yu, you must know your hundred-yuan note isn't worth anything anymore," Baba said.

Uncle Yu smiled. Others had told him the same thing. No, he was all full of confidence; how could the sheep bill not be worth anything? It was real. It was in the toe of his shoe, wasn't it?

But a pestering doubt had germinated and was growing. One day he asked Nainai for his satchel and walked into town to buy tobacco; but the shopkeeper only shook his head when he tried to pay with the sheep bill.

"That pretty money is only good for rolling your smokes with," the shopkeeper told him.

And that afternoon Baba saw the man in

town, walking with a long, drawn face, wearing a bitterness uncommon to his features. His shaved pate showed traces of perspiration.

When he returned home, Uncle Yu sat down on the edge of the kang, pulled out the sheep bill, and stared at it. He turned it over from time to time and sighed his familiar sigh. Tears squeezed out from the corners of his long, narrow eyes.

"Oh, Uncle Yu, please don't cry," folk pleaded with him. But the more they tried to comfort him, the faster the tears tumbled down.

"It was all for nothing," he said between sniffles and hiccups.

"But you made it back all in one piece from Sankeshu. Your life is more important than the money." He was deaf to their words.

After the tears had slowed to a trickle, he folded the money and, as before, placed it back inside the shoe. This time, however, he did not hand over his satchel to Nainai for safekeeping.

From time to time, when Baba went to visit the man in his room, he saw him hunched over on the kang, dumbly staring at the sheep bill and wiping away a substantial tear.

Uncle Yu worked for Baba's family through fall, winter, and spring. For several days in the summer of 1946, he was nowhere to be seen.

When he reappeared, he wore the uniform of a Nationalist soldier—a soldier of China's central government. The shirt was several sizes too small; the trousers were sizes too big. The man scratched his scalp. White flakes rained down. He smiled his shy smile and stared down at his shoes. It seemed that he had stopped grieving.

"Uncle Yu, why did you decide to become a soldier? You don't even know how to fire a gun," said Baba.

"Yes, but I won't be needing a gun. I am a cook in the army. All I'll need to know is how to light a fire under the kettle.

"And best of all, I'll be making two silver yuan a month. Silver. Real money. Not paper money."

Uncle Yu was transferred from Xinmin to neighboring Zhangwu soon after.

His unit saw fighting that winter. Heavy fighting.

The Communist troops, known as the Eighth Route Army, easily overran the entrenched Nationalists' Forty-ninth Brigade. The opposing Chinese factions had come rushing into Manchuria, each in its own fashion, in the race to fill the vacuum left by the departed Japanese.

Folk of Xinmin saw the defeated Nationalist soldiers limping on crutches or lying upon stretchers, blood frozen hard on their cotton-padded coats, when they returned from battle.

And every day, Baba strained to see Uncle Yu among the ragtag men. "He'd surely come back here if he could. This is his home," Baba said.

For a period of over five months now, Uncle Yu had been serving in the army. Dead or alive, he would have ten silver yuan in hand. Silver. Real money. Not paper money.

"THIRD BROTHER, nearly nineteen, is to be given a wife very soon. I fear I'm next," my father said to himself in the spring of 1946. "I'm seventeen now. . . . I've already heard the elders talk of pairing me up with someone.

"Who needs it!

"I can't see what's in front of my own nose; everything's so murky, what with the war. How will I find my way? Will there be a future for me? Will I have the chance to continue with school? The last thing I want is to be saddled with a wife!

"The elders—they play us young people like puppets."

It was hard for Baba to forget all the fuss and heartache over Eldest Brother's and Second Brother's marriages, the noisy, cramped celebrations that had taken place over four years before.

"That precious eldest grandson of yours—the one who studies at the university—he's courting a girl. They walk together unchaper-

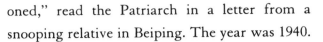

oned," read the Patriarch in a letter from a snooping relative in Beiping. The year was 1940.

The news about Eldest Brother—age nineteen, and seven years Baba's senior—struck the Patriarch over the head like a cudgel.

"He will marry the girl of my choosing in a traditional ceremony! We will have none of this newfangled Western 'free love'!" said he. In his anger, his heavy black brows seemed to stick out farther than the fur of his beaverskin hat.

"I want a big wedding celebration," Baba heard the Patriarch loudly declare, and everyone knew that there would be much trouble under the roof of the House of Yang.

The Patriarch, now in his sixties, was at the pinnacle of his power and wealth. A big wedding celebration was an opportunity for him to gather together friends and relatives separated by distance and a great number of years; he wanted to show off the splendid results of his half century of toil. Weddings were for the pleasure of the elders; they had little to do with the young folk who were to be united.

"Your mother is ill. Come home immediately," read the telegram that Eldest Brother received at school. He rushed home, leaving Beiping in New China to return to Xinmin in Japanese-occupied Manchuria.

Once home, Eldest Brother realized that he had been duped. The family refused to obtain a passport for him to return to Beiping. There came to be an unbending silence between him and the Patriarch.

A year passed, and the talk about marriage remained a most unhappy issue. But the passion that had been ignited by conflict was slowly cooled by tedious, droning reality. The exchange of letters between Elder Brother and his girlfriend far away dribbled to a sullen end.

Meanwhile, the matchmaker had come to sing the praise of a daughter from the Cao family (as everyone knows, the tongue of a matchmaker can make even a winter squash virtuous and beautiful).

"Her face is shaped like the seed of a watermelon; her brows are like the antennae of a moth; her nose is straight and smooth as jade, her waist slim as a willow wand. The daughter of Cao is a smart girl, too: one of the few women to graduate from the teachers college. Better yet, she is from a very respectable family: her father was the police chief of three counties in Guangxi Province, no less."

"Hmm, yes, sounds like she will make a suitable wife for Number One. We will bring this girl into the family," said the Patriarch.

"Do any of you know what day and age this is!" thundered Eldest Brother upon hearing of the decision made for him. He paced the room like a man condemned to the gallows.

"I will not marry a girl I've never laid eyes on. The traditional marriage is like tying two mud dolls together with a string." Eldest Brother slotted his narrow, distrustful eyes. He had fully inherited the mulish intransigence of the Yangs.

In the end, when both the Patriarch and his grandson had tired of maintaining their postures of defiance, a compromise was reached. Eldest Brother would consider marriage if allowed to see the girl first.

"What if she has a face like Zhubajie—the pig in 'Journey to the West'?" he said.

But he could not well saunter over to the Caos' and have a look at their daughter. A formal "date" had to be arranged.

Eldest Brother would be accompanied by a chaperon; the Miss Cao in question would be accompanied by another. At the agreed-upon date and time, one party would approach the meeting place from the north; the other party would approach from the south. Eldest Brother and Miss Cao would not recognize each other, of course, but the two chaperons were well acquainted.

At the appointed hour, the go-betweens herded the young people past each other on the crowded, busy street without pause—without even slowing. Eldest Brother had to base a decision of a lifetime upon an intense two seconds' worth of scrutiny.

What he saw of Miss Cao, he liked: she was uncommonly beautiful. Still, there was one other condition before he would consent to marriage:

"The wedding ceremony must be 'civilized'—it has to be modern, or I will have none of it," he said.

The Patriarch was sorely disappointed, but in the end he relented; it was better to have a modern marriage than to have no marriage at all.

The old gentleman, however, refused to attend the ceremony.

"Bah, they say the traditional marriage is uncivilized. What's so civilized about all this? The bride is dressed up all in funeral white.

"Hai, and her family is here also—her father is now giving a speech: I can hear him droning. I've never heard of in-laws coming to the wedding; they are to drop the bride off at the matchmaker's and then go home.

"And no trumpets! Only a wheezing organ that plays this mournful march. . . ." Baba saw the Patriarch sitting in his study, keeping company with old friends and aging relatives, who shook their heads in commiseration.

"I will have a traditional wedding for a grandson of mine if it's the last thing I do," said he.

Soon after Eldest Brother's wedding, the matchmaker was again seen scurrying in and out of the Patriarch's chambers.

"The beauty of the eldest daughter of the Li family causes fishes to sink and wild ducks to swoon from the sky. She is very delicate: her fingers are long and tapering, like stalks of spring onions," said the old woman to the Patriarch.

"And let me tell you, her family owns many hundreds of mu of black soil, where the output of sorghum is double that of most other regions."

The eight characters describing Miss Li's hour, day, month, and year of birth were given to a blind fortune-teller, along with those of Second Brother's. The match would be an auspicious one, the man said after long deliberation.

Second Brother—a year younger than Eldest Brother—for all his rambunctiousness, was even-tempered. To him, no issue was important enough for confrontation; he always managed to find a way around a situation to satisfy his own needs. "He's a 'nonlinear thinker,'" folk said of him. He paid little heed to all the fuss around him about finding him a bride.

Following upon the matchmaker's visits, Nainai and Yeye descended upon the House of Li to inspect their marriageable daughter.

Nainai placed the rings and bangles, gifts for Miss Li, in a box wrapped in red velvet. A pair of earrings, however, she kept inside her own pocket, for she would personally hang these upon the girl's ears.

"We must not neglect to inspect her earlobes. We can't allow a girl with skimpy earlobes to marry into the family, no matter how nice-looking she is. Girls with thin earlobes won't bring our house good fortune."

Miss Li's earlobes passed Nainai's examination; they must have been quite substantial.

A propitious day in the Month of the Twelfth Moon was chosen for the wedding.

At the auspicious hour of three in the morning, two palanquins, each borne by four carriers, wended their way to the matchmaker's house, where the bride was waiting. Their path was illuminated by big red lanterns that resembled overgrown pumpkins. Sitting inside the palanquin of the groom, which was decorated with the dragon motif, was Second Brother. Superstition dictated that the bride's phoenix palanquin must not travel empty; Baba, small and light for a thirteen-year-old, was recruited to warm the seat.

Seven trumpets rent the silence of the frigid winter morn like disputing geese; three cackling cymbals joined in the fray. Barking dogs greeted them all along the way. No one was allowed sleep.

"No, no, young'un. Don't get off till they give you the red envelope," said the palanquin bearers to Baba upon arrival. By custom, he was not to budge until he received his "bribe" money from the family of the bride.

While Second Brother was kept waiting in another room, Baba slipped into the inner chamber. His soon-to-be sister-in-law was swathed in layers of brocade. Women assisted her with her makeup, plastering on rouge as thick as that upon an opera singer's face; atop her head they settled her headdress, a mountainous mass of jiggling red pompons.

Outside, the palanquin bearers hopped about from one foot to the other like monkeys to keep warm, while blasts of white vapor issued from their mouths as they huffed on their clapping hands. The musicians blew their trumpets and clanged their cymbals to rush the bride.

Inside the house, Baba watched the matchmaker spill forty Ming dynasty coins onto a spread of red velvet cloth.

"Don't be greedy, girl," she said to the bride. "Take only half the coins and leave the rest for your old parents."

With a sweep of her hand, the bride scooped up some coins.

"Good girl. You are truly evenhanded and just," said the matchmaker. "Even though you will soon belong to another, you should not forget the house of your mother."

The music outside played with greater urgency. The matchmaker threw a large red kerchief over the head of the bride; it enveloped her like a blinding sunrise. She was helped onto her palanquin. Baba now trotted alongside.

Folk were awakened once again as the marriage party made the return journey. No one really minded the loss of sleep: they lay snug under their quilts and listened to the delicious discord, reminded of their own weddings or given an earful of the music that awaited them on some future date.

When the wedding party arrived at the House of Yang, the groom's palanquin entered the main gate, whereupon the door was quickly shut upon the bride. The patience of the future wife was to be tested; she was made to wait and wait; she was asked to curtail her temper.

"*Hao le! Hao le!*" the musicians and the palanquin bearers hollered outside the gate. "Enough! Enough! Let us in! She will be a du-tiful daughter-in-law! She has displayed great forbearance! Let us in!" They raised a big racket. Finally, the door swung open.

But the bride's palanquin was soon arrested at the inner gate.

"*Hao le! Hao le!*" they yelled once again. "She will make a tolerant wife!" (In reality, the patience tested was that of the palanquin bearers: they wished to deposit their burdens quickly and return home to sleep.) After a while, the inner gate also swung open.

Lanterns glowed faintly in the darkness. At the center of the courtyard, upon a red carpet, stood a table set with two red candles and an incense urn.

Next to the table was a large wooden box, whose opening had been sealed with red paper; the lever of a scale had broken through the seal and was planted in the sorghum contained within; a pan hung from the hook of the scale: "The hook cannot be without the pan, just as the old woman cannot do without her old man," was the saying—a wish for a harmonious life for the young couple.

The bride was helped down from her palanquin and led to stand silently before the table. Second Brother, the groom, stood to her left, in his skullcap and marriage robe. The musicians gathered behind the pair as the candles and incense were lit in honor of Heaven and Earth. Baba heard a rooster crow, though it was still hours before dawn.

"The God of Happiness is in the east!" the man hired to perform the marriage rites cried for all to hear.

Second Brother kowtowed three times facing east.

"The God of Good Fortune is in the south!"

Second Brother kowtowed three times facing south.

And with this, the simple ceremony was ended: Heaven and Earth had acknowledged the union.

The newlyweds were led to the bridal chamber. Tagging along as always, Baba saw that the windows and walls had been newly papered, and a curtain, embroidered with a dragon and a phoenix, cascaded from the ceiling before the kang.

When the curtain was parted, a large grain-filled sack was revealed to have been set upon the kang. The bride, with her head still veiled, was made to perch upon the sack, following a custom known as "meditating upon good fortune."

The trumpets and cymbals were silenced. The family and guests sat in the rooms, talking quietly, sipping tea, awaiting the dawn, which would announce the commencement of three days of noisy celebration.

When Old Man Sun finally poked his head out of the east, the bride was liberated from her sitting exercise. Only then was the groom allowed to remove her head covering.

According to strict rule, this was to be the first time the groom would gaze upon the face of his bride, but Second Brother, the "nonlinear thinker," had long been secretly courting Miss Li.

Shortly after the match had been arranged,

he had accosted her in town and had invited her out to dine many a time. He was well aware that she was no shrinking violet and was nobody's fool: she was a progressive-minded young woman, a social worker for the city of Xinmin.

When Second Brother removed her head covering, she smiled demurely, but Baba guessed she was not blushing under her rouge at the sight of the groom. Baba had known of their trysts all the while. He had strung along after them to restaurants and clamored to be fed as the price for not tattling.

Soon began the bride's endless, dizzying rounds of reverential bows to all her new relatives.

For the next several days, the newlyweds were not given rest; family and friends played pranks, placing dates and chestnuts—their names a homonym for "the early arrival of children"—in their bed, which they had to shake out nightly.

When the fourth morning of the marriage arrived, the bride, according to custom, returned to her mother's house for the day, trailed by the unshakable guests; and there, also, the revelers ate like locusts.

By the fifth morning, most of the guests had departed the House of Yang (although some stayed more than a month), leaving the pair to begin their new life together.

Now that the Patriarch had had his big traditional wedding, he troubled himself no more with the marriage affairs of his remaining grandsons.

It was nearly four years after Second Brother's wedding that Baba heard Nainai worrying over matters concerning his third brother's impending marriage.

"Third Son is a bit of a cabbagehead," she said. "He will need a strong woman to take care of him."

Baba knew this to be true; his brother had been prey to school bullies, and it was he, the scrappy younger one, who had to fend off his brother's tormentors. Third Brother preferred the company of barnyard animals, especially plodding old draft animals, to human beings. "Mother is right, he is a cabbagehead," Baba said to himself, "but Third Brother is the most genuine of our disorderly lot."

When the Japanese surrendered in the summer of 1945, the "Big Noses," as folk dubbed the Russians, arrived and began systematically looting rich, industrial Manchuria. Once the Russians left the scene, the Communists and the Nationalists battled for control. All the while, the redbeards again proliferated and preyed upon folk in the countryside, gobbling up the morsels dropped by the much larger hunters. Third Brother's marriage would take place against this somber backdrop.

Nainai agreed, sight unseen, to a peasant girl for her third son; she had no heart for details such as inspecting a girl's earlobes.

The House of Zhang was in a big hurry to marry off their daughter: there was no telling what would happen to a maiden with all the hungry, warring men running loose.

Her folk rushed her, like perishable goods, to the House of Yang, riding in the back of a horse-drawn wagon, wearing flowers in her hair.

The groom made the rounds of kowtows to Heaven and Earth; his plump, box-faced bride made the rounds of bows to the elders. Feast and celebration followed, but it was a simple affair, which ended by sunset.

"No, the last thing in the world I need now is to take care of a wife. Under the current circumstances, I can't even be sure I'll be able to take care of myself," my father said in 1946, during the days of upheaval.

But marriage was not to be in the immediate picture for him: the escalating war would soon sweep away everything—even the threat of a traditional arranged marriage.

It would not be until Baba was older, after he had walked thousands of miles and crossed the water, and had come to settle on an island of relative peace, that he would find his mate. Mama.

Her family would set the dog and the gander on the penniless refugee, but my father would whisk her away with him anyway.

On their wedding day, the two of them would wear shoes with holes but a clean shirt and blouse. They would stand in a courtroom along with thirty other couples, awaiting the performance of a civil ceremony.

En masse, the gathering would bow once to the judge. En masse, man and woman would bow once to each other.

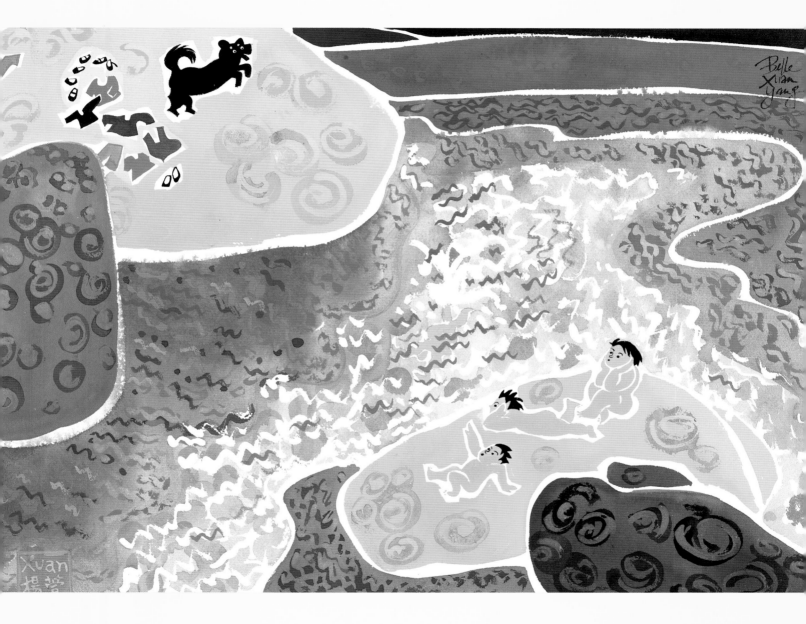

THE EVENING OF Third Brother's wedding, in the spring of 1946, seemed strangely silent to my father. How different it was in the time of Eldest Brother's wedding, Baba thought. The darkness was dressed in layers of night sounds, the howling of the neighbors' dogs . . . and yes, also the familiar bark of Big Black in the yard.

Big Black started out in this world small. The pup was no bigger than a corn muffin. Just like a glossy little bear, thought twelve-year-old Baba as he watched the creature toddle on soft legs, head all shaky and trembling.

"I'll take this guy with the four eyes," Baba said, choosing him from among a litter of six. With two tan dabs on his brow, he had a wise, thoughtful look about him.

The grown-ups ground their teeth in despair, for in the night, the pup, mewling for his mother, disturbed their dreams. Baba welcomed him under his quilt, and upon finding reassurance within the womblike wrap, he licked Baba's neck and chin.

Big Black was weaned on sorghum porridge. When he was one month old, Baba built him a house of mud bricks and lined the inside with the horses' hay. He was true to his name, for he sent the bricks scattering four times as he outgrew his home.

He accompanied his young master everywhere. As Baba ran on the snow-mantled grounds of the South Garden early in the morning, he followed with ears flopping, clenching a willow branch between his massive jaws. In the summertime, when the boys swam in the river Liao, he stood guard over their clothes on the bank, whimpering, his eyes begging to join them when they had been too long in the water.

On such outings, Baba always gave an even half of his onion pancakes to his four-eyed companion, whose keen nose had already guessed what they would be eating at midday. At dusk, the family was relieved to see Big Black's electric-tailed return, for his presence told them that the children would soon be home.

The year the down on Baba's face turned to whiskers and Big Black had reached his biggest, the gods struck down Zhang, the family's good neighbor and tenant.

The man was a straight-boned, handsome fellow of forty-five who was the descendant of a line of healers; his art was at a level above that of a village herbalist but below that of a physician in the city. He was a learned man with an artistic bent, displaying an admirable calligraphic hand.

Zhang traveled the country roads, plying his trade in the various villages for periods ranging up to two months. He wore a scholarly robe and jangled his iron *chuanling,* a hollow, fist-size ring containing iron beads. The villagers, upon hearing the *ga-lang, ga-lang, ga-lang,* knew that a healer had arrived.

At the end of each of his journeys, Zhang returned home with a satchel full of money, but he and his wife and their two sons lived unpretentiously on the squash and eggplants from their own garden. Baba, following his keen nose, would often invite himself to their table at sup-pertime to listen to the adventures of the traveling doctor.

When his eldest turned twenty-one, Zhang decided to take the young man along with him on an excursion, wishing to pass on his knowledge of the healing arts to the next generation. They crossed the river Liao to reach the hamlet of Daming on the southern bank. The son respectfully followed behind his father, holding on to the handles of the leather case that contained vials of precious herbs.

The villagers of Daming invited the healer into their homes. For one suffering a sore throat, Zhang tapped a smidgen of white powder into one end of a thin metal straw and blew the bitter stuff into the throat of the gape-mouthed patient; the medicine contained camphor, "sweet grass," and ginger. For one suffering the pain and embarrassment of bounteous flatulence, he prescribed five little black pills, five times a day; the pungent concoction contained wood tar and licorice, its odor remaining upon his hands for days even after numerous scrubbings. For one afflicted with a facial boil, Zhang brought out his expedient lancet. If the good doctor's skills could not cure the man, they certainly would not kill him either. He was paid what his patients deemed fair.

The journey to Daming had been profitable: Zhang had relieved the arthritic joints of the mayor and had been generously compensated. The father and son began their homeward journey.

But to their dismay, the Liao had become wrathful, swollen by rains upriver. The water churned all around the ferry as it attempted to return to the northern shore. To make things worse, the wind had kicked up; the bent willows along the flooded banks tossed like hair. Perhaps the passengers had been distracted by some object bobbing in the unruly water; no one can now recall. But their sudden rush to one side capsized the vessel. The son managed to stay afloat by grabbing onto the boat as it was carried downstream. He returned home alone.

When a man dies, his soul enters *feng du cheng,* the ghost city. On the seventh day, the soul ascends a high platform and gazes upon the man's native village. If the proper funeral rites have been performed, his soul will leave the platform and either climb to Heaven or descend to Hell (there to be punished and to begin its transmigration into the body of a lowly animal). But if his family has failed to perform the last rites, his soul is condemned to haunt his old abode.

As Zhang's body had not been found along the banks of the Liao, his family continued to harbor hope of his return.

Seven days after the calamity, just after midnight, Big Black began to bark. It was not the aggressive snapping sound of challenging another dog, nor was it the sluggish howling of warning off a two-legged intruder. No, the townsfolk said, it was the not-so-fast, not-so-slow cadence of a dog barking at forces invisible to the living.

"Shhh, quiet, boy. Quiet, Big Black. You mustn't waken everyone," Baba said. But in spite of the reassuring pats and admonishments, Big

Black persisted in his doleful cries. Occasionally he stopped, cocked his massive head, and looked steadily at Baba with his four eyes.

"Do not fret, young master, I know what I'm doing," he seemed to say. "There are things in this world you'll never be able to comprehend."

He was joined by another family pet, a

smaller, yellow dog, and the two animals yawped and yammered, pointing their noses toward the southeast corner of the courtyard, where the Zhangs lived.

On the third night of this queer occurrence, the Patriarch of the House of Yang assumed his Daoist posture of meditation. His spirit escaped from the top of his head and flew into the damp night air, where, above the rooftop of the Zhangs', the old gentleman's spirit encountered the wavering, immaterial form of a boat—one minute visible, the next minute not. At the stern of the spectral boat hovered the figure of a man, whose milky blue face was swollen as tight as a drum; from his long, disheveled hair rolled beads of brown water.

After the Patriarch told him of this vision, Baba did not dare venture into the yard to hush Big Black; he cracked the window open an inch to peer out from the safety within.

"Tomorrow go tell the wife of Zhang that her husband is no longer among the living," the Patriarch said to him. "Tell her to send for the monks. They must perform the last rites, or no one will be at peace."

A fortnight after the healer's disappearance into the waters of the Liao, nine monks in gray, maroon, and gold settled cross-legged upon the kang in his home, their figures dissolving into the heavy incense smoke that choked the room; they chanted Buddhist scriptures and banged on the gong and drum from noon until midnight as the family kowtowed, made offerings of food, lit candles, and burned paper spirit money for the dead.

A fat-faced moon presided over the silence once the clamorous rites had come to an end. Big Black was in his house of mud bricks, his front paws folded neatly beneath his head, his four eyes closed in sleep.

When Baba was nearly seventeen and Big Black was at the handsome, rambunctious age of five, the Japanese surrendered; in that autumn of 1945, Chinese Communist soldiers seeped into the city.

Their immediate order of business was to

round up the dogs. They tied their four legs together and hurled them onto the backs of trucks.

"Dogs are the servants of the feudal lords," they said. What they did not say was that their soldiers prowled in the darkness, when the senses of the dogs were at their keenest.

Within a few days, all the dogs in town had vanished. The silence disturbed everyone's dreams.

"DEVILS WILL RULE the Middle Kingdom. Make ready, I say! Surrender all worldly illusions—relinquish all you possess! Make ready! Make ready!" These words, and the peculiar fellow who uttered them, my father remembered in the days of mourning for Big Black.

Although folk had called him "Idiot Yuan" to his face, it was without malice.

"Ah, Idiot Yuan, I was hoping you'd come. Welcome, old friend," Baba had often heard the Patriarch say. And in reply, out of the man's wide, frog mouth would come empty laughter, sounding like seedpods rattling in the wind.

Idiot Yuan wore a silk skullcap atop a spray of long hair that was cut bluntly at the shoulders—hair so black it absorbed all light. He sniffled and snuffled, fluid always threatening to slide out of his nose and down his stringy beard. His big, bloodshot eyes were shaded by protrusive brow ridges, above which vertical veins, like two purple cords, throbbed. The man was poor in expressions, hanging only one upon

his swarthy face: that of a foolish half-smile.

Baba guessed that he made his bed in some cobwebbed corner of the Temple to the King of Hell or of any number of other shrines in Xinmin.

Children always seemed to know of his whereabouts. They followed him as he shuffled through the streets, tagging along at a safe distance, chanting: "Here he comes! Yuan the Idiot! Idiot Yuan!"

The man paid them little attention; he walked with his eyes focused on something beyond eternity. Occasionally he would turn around and wave his cane distractedly in the air, as if to shoo away gnats. The children, baiting him for just such a reaction, squawked and squealed in delicious fear. The man continued on his way.

In what manner Idiot Yuan made a living, no one was certain. He was never seen to beg. Neither had he ever been accused of stealing.

One summer, Baba saw him dressed in tattered clothes, freelancing as a *kailugui*—the devil who clears the way—dancing and grimacing at the head of a rich man's funeral procession to frighten away the multitude of gawkers who blocked the way.

This was the only occasion on which Baba had ever seen the man take on a different demeanor: his face was painted green, his eyes bulged, and he gnashed his teeth.

Ga-ga-ga, he sounded with a long stick on a block of wood as he hopped about ahead of the trumpeters, the retinue of murmuring monks, and the ornate coffin, crafted from the most expensive cedar and borne by sixteen pallbearers.

Back in the winter of 1942, at the wedding of Eldest Brother, as Baba and a sister sat down at one of the many banquet tables to eat, Idiot Yuan was ushered into the hall. To the children's great dismay, the man was given a seat at their table. The two of them each grabbed a dish within their reach and scooted to the opposite end.

Yuan the Idiot made much noise over his bowl: he slurped and lapped away at his soup.

His chopsticks were all tangled up in his beard. Occasionally he paused, raised his eyes to stare blankly at the children, and laughed that empty, rattling laughter of his, seeming as if he had only just noticed their company.

The children, having lost much of their appetite, ate hurriedly and left the man alone at the table, to mutter Daoist prayers as he savored his food.

"Why does Grandfather always invite this man? Doesn't he notice how filthy he is?" Baba said.

"He reeks of a fox den," his sister answered.

But Idiot Yuan was greatly admired by the Patriarch—a man who himself possessed *weiyan,* an aura so imposing that his silent presence was enough to clear a path in a crowded railway station; army officers offered up their seats when the stately old gentleman entered their train compartment.

Though impatient with ill manners, the Patriarch was strangely blind to Idiot Yuan's many nasty habits.

At what point the two became friends, Baba did not know; most likely when the Patriarch had come to accumulate great wealth, prestige, and power, and was easing into his old age, surrounded by his grown children and their host of little ones; that is, when he began to ensconce himself in the study of Daoism.

Each autumn, when the frost was upon the eggplant, Idiot Yuan came to visit. The first thing he did upon entering the House of Yang was to show his respect to the family by praying at their altar to Buddha.

"Come in. Come in, dear friend," the Patriarch would say as he showed the man into his study, inviting him to take a seat upon one of the "eight immortal chairs" as an honored guest.

"Eh, Granddaddy," Idiot Yuan would say. "The steely winds of autumn are again upon us. . . ." This signaled that he had come for his winter clothes.

As in the previous years, the Patriarch had set aside a heavy coat, a padded jacket, and a pair of trousers to see the man through winter.

By summer, however, Idiot Yuan would have sold everything.

Together, the two men talked for hours, delving into the mystery of the Dao.

As Idiot Yuan spoke, his right arm plunged down the collar of his jacket and traveled far and wide upon his person in search of vermin. Once, Baba saw him pluck out a louse, take off his skullcap, plant the creature upon the top of his head, and then replace the cap.

"Why didn't you smash it between your fingernails?" asked Baba. "Why didn't you kill it!"

"*Sui tu bu fu,*" the man replied. "That varmint will have trouble acclimating to the water and soil of its new home and will die a most peaceful, natural death."

The Patriarch, who was fastidious in all his habits, stroked his fine white beard and laughed, the corners of his eyes crinkling.

Sometimes the two men sat facing each other with eyes closed: they were conversing spirit-to-spirit; what remained seated were only the husks, their souls having departed to hover somewhere above their heads and below the ceiling.

When his soul vacated his body, Idiot Yuan was able to see a person's previous incarnations.

"Tell me where my soul has journeyed from," said the Patriarch.

Idiot Yuan crossed his eyes, the twin purple veins upon his forehead throbbing violently; then he slowly closed his eyes to meditate.

"You are the fortieth incarnation of Tang Minghuang, Granddaddy, the emperor who reigned during the glory days of the Tang dynasty." (This revelation, of course, appealed to the Patriarch immensely.)

"Tell us what these two little radish heads were," the Patriarch said, pointing to Baba and his third brother, who were allowed the privilege of entering the study to boil water and pour tea.

Again Idiot Yuan crossed his eyes and meditated.

"Heh heh, ha ha. This one here was the boy attendant who sprouted wings, turned into a

crane, and ran away from Old Man Longevity."
He patted Baba on the head with his dark hands.

"And that one there was a wild goose."

Baba was baffled. How could he have known? How could he have reached the same conclusions? Why, not long ago, their grandfather meditated on their pasts and had the exact same visions. Perhaps there was something to all this. . . .

Not only was Idiot Yuan able to see the past; he was also able to look into the future.

"Old Granddaddy," he said in a low voice on a later visit, "last night, when the Three Stars"—Orion's belt—"were directly overhead at midnight, I saw the gates of Hell busted down and all the hungry devils come pouring out. There will be madness under Heaven real soon, I tell you. Demons will claim dominion over the Middle Kingdom. Make ready, I say! Surrender all earthly illusions—relinquish everything! Be rid of the wealth that will come to be your bane. Make ready! Make ready!"

One spring day, in the year before the Japanese surrender, as a wee breeze whispered into the ears of the corn, two strangers were seen traveling the highway into town. Both were dressed in rags, in the manner of mendicants. One had wild hair, long and all atangle, and limped along with a crutch under one arm; the other, whose pate was shaven, swung a long, gnarled staff.

"We have searched for you the world over, Brother Yuan," the hobbling one was overheard to say when they encountered Yuan at a bend in the road. "The Master is anxiously awaiting your return."

"Yes, the Master says you have been gone too long. Your time here is up. You've done enough," said the bald one.

Yuan the Idiot made no reply. He only laughed as if the wind had addled his brain.

At dusk, the threesome were seen inching along the highway, their silhouettes tiny and black against the semicircle of the setting sun.

And that was the last day that anyone in Xinmin was to hear the fantastic laughter of Idiot Yuan.

"No need to make fun of him—there's more to the man than you guess," said the Patriarch to Baba. That fall, the man did not arrive at the House of Yang to claim his winter clothing.

"Someday, when I am ready," my father heard the Patriarch mutter to himself, "when I am willing to renounce my all—I will follow him on the road to the Western Paradise."

Little did the Patriarch know he would not have the time to make ready. The gates of Hell would be busted down before too long.

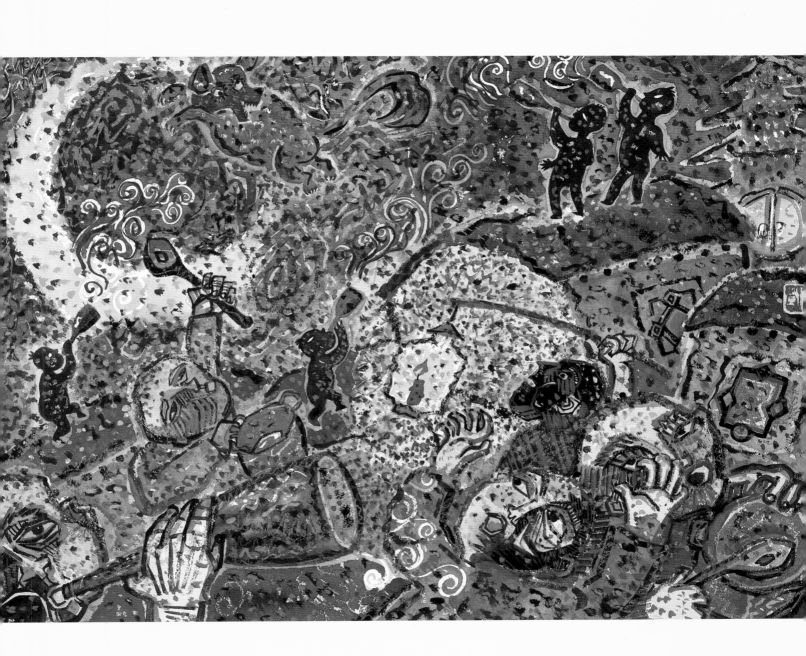

WHEN MY FATHER was thirteen, the Japanese had ordered all the children at school to paint posters depicting Churchill as a pumpkin, Roosevelt as a radish, and Chiang Kai-shek as an eggplant, their faces plastered with little white crosses of bandages: the Japanese were boasting of the beating they had administered to their foes. The posters were put up on the walls of the school and throughout Baba's hometown.

"Huh, Tojo, the Japanese Premier, is no prettier than these three. His head is like an egg with spectacles. Egg will surely lose against the joint forces of pumpkin, radish, and eggplant," folk had muttered under their breaths.

"Life will be good when the Japanese are gone. Manchuria will once again be our own," they said.

But after the atomic bombs were released on Japan in August of 1945, peace did not come for the Manchurians.

Idiot Yuan had vanished, but his prognostication of "madness under Heaven" sounded with greater urgency inside Baba's head; now it rattled with truth.

Immediately upon the scene of the Japanese defeat, the Soviet Russians arrived in Manchuria, like vultures drawn by the smell of death. The unknowing Chinese populace welcomed them as liberators.

(At the conference in Yalta earlier that year, Roosevelt, Churchill, and Stalin had secretly agreed upon the reestablishment of the Russian presence in Manchuria in return for Russian help against the Japanese.)

On the afternoon the Russians were to arrive in Xinmin, Baba waited at the North Gate of the city, among the welcoming crowd organized by the local business association.

In the distance, a rolling yellow thunderhead of dust was all that could be seen of the approach of the Russian host, a fragment of the army entering from Mongolia.

Russian tanks rumbled into the narrow streets. They were big, ugly things, their welded joints unfinished in the great hurry for the lunge into Asia and clearly visible like fresh scars.

Folk waved and cheered when the swart Russians with thick arms and thicker legs climbed out of the tanks and stepped off jeeps and motorcycles. Their faces and vehicles were caked with pale yellow dirt, looking as if men and machine had been molded from the soil of the steppe.

The citizens of Xinmin reached out to shake their liberators' hands. But instead of a return grasp of friendship, the Russians, with darting eyes, reached out with their hands to snatch watches from the wrists and fountain pens from the shirt pockets of the astounded welcomers. It was no wonder: decades later, Baba would learn that these soldiers were recruited from among criminals in the prison camps of Siberia.

"The Big Noses are here! The Big Noses are here! But they've stripped us bare of our valuables!" cried the panicked, stampeding masses. A wave of hysteria spread through the community. Shopkeepers clanged shut and bolted their steel doors.

The Russians began methodically to plunder Manchuria of machinery and stores of manufactured goods. Factories were removed wholesale.

Folk said it was as if the clock had been turned back two hundred years: electric trolleys rusted at the depots, for the generators had been carried off to Russia; telephones were cut off; radio stations were shut down; newspapers could not be published; the feeble yellow light of makeshift lamps—rice bowls containing soybean oil, with strings for wicks—cast uncanny shadows.

No one ventured out at night. Many an evening, as the people sat in the darkness, they heard the noises of entire houses as they came crashing down, sounding like breaking bones, ripping sinews; the buildings were collapsed by the careless maneuvers of Russian tanks in the narrow streets.

Girls who worked outside the home during the day cut their long braids to deflect the gaze of predatory soldiers.

One evening, after Baba's family had finished supper, a piercing scream was heard in the North Garden. When the men ran out back, they found a solitary Russian soldier ramming a tall pile of kindling with the butt of his rifle.

A fifteen-year-old girl, whose family ran the neighborhood bathhouse, had tried to hide from the man under the cone of kindling but had been flushed out. She was unhurt but was so frightened she lay stretched out on the ground, her body stiffened like a ceramic doll.

The soldier found himself surrounded by glaring men who encircled him with knives, shovels, and hoes.

A few flinty stars clasped the sky. The only noise was the soft whimper of the girl!

The Russian soldier shrank into himself. The predator had become prey. He made unfamiliar noises and gestured, perhaps to say: "I've lost my way. I am far from home. . . ." He was escorted out the garden gate.

Meanwhile, the grannies, aunties, mothers, and sisters of the House of Yang had climbed behind a false wall, to hide from what they believed was the sure onslaught of a barbaric horde.

"The danger's over! You can all come out now!" Baba called to them. But they maintained a tight cluster in the dark and refused to show themselves. It was many hours before they emerged, one by one, like a covey of quail darting out from the shrubbery.

In the Middle Kingdom, since an age that the rivers and hills have trouble remembering, when a gloom was cast over the sky by a solar or lunar eclipse, folk said the hungry "Heavenly Dog" was to blame. To force the monster to disgorge, folk screamed and hollered, their cries rising fierce and shrill over the incessant banging of basins, tubs, and pans. This remedy never failed to bring back the sun or moon.

Now that the Big Noses were darkening the sky with their misdeeds, the people brought out their only weapons. Wherever trouble occurred in the night, neighbors orchestrated a racket to frighten away the marauders.

No one knew what clever person first came up with the idea, but with the arrival of the Russians, the cry of horns made from big glass bottles whose bottoms had been cut away was heard above the din of the pots and pans. It was disquieting to be awakened in the middle of the night by their low wailing. When the deep-throated call of a horn sounded desperately from a rooftop in the distance, another replied, followed by yet another: each family like an island in a turbid black sea, but united in defense against a common enemy. The sky over Xinmin sang with the long, hollow moans, which starched the hairs on the backs of necks, unsettled nerves, caused friends and foes alike to shiver in mild weather. In no time, the entire city was sounding alarms in the night.

Many a night, Baba accompanied his third brother, whose clever hands had fashioned several of the horns, on the rooftop to echo the distant alarm.

The people had nothing else; only these crude instruments to wage war against the Big Noses. But the pots, pans, basins, and horns were effective only in the dark.

When Baba's sharp ears caught the sound of cries and gunshots on North Street one Septem-

ber day, he ran, against the admonishments of his family, to see what the commotion was about.

Several wounded men were being carried away, and a boy about Baba's age lay at the entrance to an alley. Sun and sweat glistened on the boy's darkened face. A clenched hand attempted to stop the blood that oozed from his shirt and pooled black on his belly. A crowd had been standing on the street, watching the movements of the Russians, satisfying their curiosity about men with pale eyes like blue glass and hair the color of withered grass, when the soldiers had opened fire.

Following close upon the heels of the Russians in that autumn of 1945 came Chinese soldiers; but they were not the troops of the Central Government.

They did not appear in contingents but trickled into town in groups of four or five. It was the first time women soldiers were seen—handsome women with vigorous strides, who wore their hair bobbed; over their olive-green uniforms they had fastened wide belts with holsters in which they carried pistols adorned with brash red sashes.

The Russians gave the arms surrendered by the Japanese to these men and women, who called themselves soldiers of the Eighth Route Army. These soldiers told the people they were followers of Communism.

What is Communism? the people asked.

They told the people they believed in Mao Zedong.

Who is Mao? We have only heard of Chiang, head of the Central Government, the people replied.

The Communists set up the Sino-Soviet Friendship Society and posted notices all over town to allay fears. "All will be well under Communism. The people must go back to work; the people must carry on with their lives as before," these read.

Who could possibly trust those who would call the Russians friends? the people whispered. The men and women of Manchuria stared across the plains, straining until their eyes stung, waiting for deliverance, waiting for the arrival of the troops of the Central Government. They waited with their hearts thundering in a wild emptiness.

Late that season, just before the first snowfall, the Nationalists finally did come. They had fought all the way from Shanhaiguan, just south of the Great Wall, against the Communists.

The first to arrive were the petite, dark men from Guangxi Province, deep in the south. They chattered away in a staccato dialect, indecipherable to the Mandarin-speakers of Manchuria. They unloaded weapons from the trains with quickness and agility. Upon their thin frames hung uniforms cut for American soldiers; it looked as if the uniforms were wearing them instead.

The Manchurians watched in awe as these *houzi bing*—monkey soldiers—in big black rubber boots bumped around town in jeeps.

"Mother of mine! The Nationalists have sent monkeys!" they exclaimed. "Chiang Kai-shek must be a man of powerful magic to be able to train monkeys to fight." And monkeys they really believed them to be, until closer inspection.

The Nationalists continued to fight northward toward Shenyang, Changchun, and Jilin.

More recruits arrived from distant provinces. They came in far greater numbers than the Communists, who by this time had dissolved back into the countryside.

When the public buildings were filled and could not quarter more troops, the Nationalist soldiers invaded private homes.

"Jun min he zuo"—Soldiers and the people will work hand in hand—was their slogan.

In addition to bearing the burden of sheltering the troops, each family was ordered to send one member to help dig the trenches that would ring the city in defense against the Communists. Each person was responsible for bringing his own tools and provisions.

As Baba labored with the men to dig the trenches south of his home—sweat soaking through his winter clothes and stinging his eyes—the soldiers stood arms akimbo above them, cursing and scolding.

The corruption of the Nationalists quickly became evident: at roll call, civilians were made to stand in for troops that existed only on paper. A squad that numbered twelve had in reality perhaps seven or eight men. Leaders profited from the extra money, food, and clothing that they received.

It was dangerous to serve as a stand-in, as simpleminded Third Brother was coerced into doing. A great many were abducted to serve as transport coolies in distant regions. Luckily, Third Brother managed to get home.

The Nationalists initially said they would pay for the livestock that they took from the families in whose homes they were quartered, but in the end, they helped themselves to everything freely, like ferrets in the chicken coop.

Neighbor Wang's precious few birds were taken from him by the soldiers. When Baba accompanied the man to seek recompense, the sergeant said:

"Are you a man?"

"Yes, of course," said Wang.

"Are the soldiers men?"

"Yes, of course."

"Do you like to eat chicken?" demanded the sergeant.

"Certainly."

"Well, since the soldiers are men, it should be apparent that they like to eat chicken as much as you do. So what crime have they committed?" And that was the end of the matter.

The two horses that remained to the House of Yang were "borrowed" and never returned (how was the family to mill their grain?). They had gone the way of the chickens, ducks, geese, and pigs. Soon the only creatures stirring in the yard were the family members themselves.

As the Communists in the surrounding countryside cut rail lines (most often, they removed the tracks in the night and buried them), the shipments of food came rarely; the grain in the silos diminished alarmingly.

Food drops were made by Nationalist fliers from Hebei Province, but the wind carried much of it into Communist territory.

When fuel supplies ran low, trees everywhere disappeared so swiftly, they seemed to have been plucked like flowers by ground squirrels. Soldiers at the House of Yang carried out furniture and tore out the ornate latticework above the windows, doors, thresholds, rafters, and beams for firewood.

Human beings received no better treatment than the tables and chairs. Soldiers kicked men on the streets. Vendors bore the brunt of their rage.

When the stranglehold of the Communists on the cities tightened further, the Nationalists were like rats caught in a sack. Having declared martial law upon arrival, they meted out punishments to the citizens ever more brutally.

Baba saw a man in a greasy brown hat and padded jacket, whose arms had been tied behind him, paraded on the street. A placard hung from his wrists. "Grain bandit," it read. Men accused of such crimes were summarily shot.

As the fighting intensified through the year 1946, many Nationalist leaders abandoned the battle and flew south to Beiping or Nanjing with their loot.

In the *Northeast People's Daily,* there was a cartoon that depicted a huge spiderweb from which a sparrow had just escaped; gnats, flies, and other small creatures, however, were caught in the sticky strands: the sparrow represented the government officials; the flies and gnats, the common people.

Meanwhile, under the shroud of darkness, the Communists continued to make forays against the besieged Nationalists. The direction of their attack varied nightly; they fired a few rounds into the cities and then quickly seeped back into the countryside.

The spooked Nationalist troops fired round after round in the early-morning hours, their gunfire sounding like the rush of wind on a blustery night. Flares and tracers lit up the sky. The smell of gunpowder choked the air. The rolling boom of cannon fire killed no enemy; it only served to crush the spirit of the people with its terrifying sound. The Nationalists wasted most of their ammunition swatting at ghosts.

And in the countryside, the Communists began their extermination of the landowners. Many of Baba's relatives suffered at their hands. In the winter of '46, those who were able to escape streamed into the cities.

"My son—they tied him up as he was teaching class, led him like a dog to kneel at the village gate. Then they shot him," his old mother, a kinswoman, told the House of Yang. She wept day and night and terrorized the family with tales of executions.

"My brother! My brother is dead!" Baba's sister-in-law cried. "They tossed a grenade through the window. It rolled and exploded beneath his bed. He screamed and struggled a few feet before collapsing. When I turned him over, I saw that he had no face. Why my brother? Of the dozens sheltered in the house, why him! Heaven above, tell me, why my brother!"

Manchuria was a land of wide-open spaces. Unlike the south, it had plentiful land. Much of it lay unclaimed. A man who worked and saved for a few years was able to become a landowner. The Communists' claim of a just war of the oppressed landless against the venal landed gentry was far from the truth.

The Communists knew men's hearts: the desire for immediate gratification. They held open the door and said, "Go ahead—it's yours for the taking. Why should they have it and not you? Why toil for it? Kill them and take it." The Communists did not bloody their own hands; they manipulated others into serving as executioners.

When the throats had been slit, the backs stabbed, the homes and storages ransacked, the Communists magnified the backwash of fear and guilt.

"Now that your hands are red with blood, the landowners will return with the help of the Nationalists to have their revenge," they said. "Don't doubt this for a minute. You'd best stick with us." The ranks of the Communists swelled.

Most men had not been able to see beyond the lulling string of days and fled only after violence and destruction became fact; but a few prescient ones among them had seen the approaching days of fury and been prepared.

A wealthy kinsman—the first person to fly about on Xinmin's dusty roads on a fashionable "farting mule"—a motorcycle—sold his estate and various properties soon after the arrival of the Russians. He did not want money but, instead, asked for payment in grain. This he requested Baba's family to store for him in their silos. Then he left Xinmin for Shenyang, the capital of the province.

In the winter of '46, when Shenyang came under siege and food supplies ran low, the relative made huge profits from the sale of the grain to the beleaguered city.

He asked Baba, nearly eighteen, to handle the transactions for him. Baba had graduated from high school over a year before and had been attending the Shenyang Polytechnic during the week, returning to Xinmin at week's end as long as the rail lines had remained open. He therefore knew his way around both Shenyang and Xinmin and was familiar with the shuttle back and forth.

Generally, the trains were running every ten days between the two cities (it took that long for the Nationalists to repair the tracks after sabotage). When the lines were open, the people from Shenyang rushed to buy what little grain was left in Xinmin, which in peacetime served as the market for raw materials and foodstuffs from the countryside. With each successive sabotage of the railway, the price of grain shot up dramatically.

Baba hid stacks of bills in his book bags on his several trips to his kinsman in Shenyang to deliver the money. No one suspected a student of traveling with such large sums of cash.

Inflation was great; the relative bought gold with the money immediately.

"How should I pay you for all your help?" the man asked Baba when his job had been completed.

"I'll take my payment in grain from what remains at the bottom of the silos. As in Shenyang, food from the countryside now can no longer reach Xinmin. There's hardly anything for the family to eat.

"The little ones suffer the most: I found my nephew has become night blind from hunger. 'Catch this, Little Yan,' I said to the toddler. He could not find the ball that I had tossed between his legs."

As the flood tide of refugees from the countryside with their narratives of death poured into Xinmin, folk there grew increasingly fearful for their own lives. They, in turn, converged upon heavily garrisoned Shenyang, seeking protection. Baba arranged housing there for the Patriarch, the womenfolk, and the younger family members.

In these days of chaos, he was already too old to hide under parental wings, yet still too young to have to bear the weight of the responsibilities fallen upon his shoulders by default. Those who should have borne the weight had gone ahead to Shenyang, concerned only with their own survival. In time of peace and prosperity, they had all laughed and celebrated as one, but now, in time of disquiet, it was easy to see how tenuously they had been bound to one another. The House of Yang came crashing down.

Yeye had been living alone in Shenyang for over a year: once the Japanese had been defeated and Manchukuo had collapsed, he willingly returned to work for the legitimate Chinese government in the province's capital. Although he had made a departure from a life of self-imposed unemployment and leisure, his overwhelming aspiration remained to attain enlightenment. When not at his office, he spent his hours at home in meditation, making sniffing noises as he circulated *qi* through his body. He said he wanted to abandon this world of illusions. What he did was abandon his duties: he had forsaken Nainai and his children in Xinmin, to fend for themselves.

In the spring of 1947, when the last of the grain had been consumed at home, Baba gathered his mother, his two younger sisters, and a baby brother, and together they boarded the rare train to Shenyang.

Yeye was furious when he saw them, his face steely and bloodless. "Why do you bring everyone here?" he said to Baba. "There is food and shelter in Xinmin!"

"You are blind, Father. If you had cared enough to go home, you would see that we have no home. This is no time for you to be concerned only with your own personal comfort," Baba spoke in anger to his parent for the first time.

"Don't you realize the destruction, Father? The Nationalists have eaten away the buildings like termites. Communist fire lands in the North Garden almost daily. We've had to pry open the floorboards in the silos to sweep up what fell through the holes that the mice chewed in the planks.

"Here in Shenyang, there is still food in the silos, however little there may be. Here, the Nationalist troops still offer some protection—though brutal, they at least do not mean to slaughter us. Here, the family may yet survive."

He took one last look at his mother; strands of hair, just hinting of silver, strayed across her cheeks. Nainai's eyes said everything: "How I wish I could protect you as I did when you were three, when the Japanese bombs landed south of the Western Marsh. But I am helpless now. How could I possibly dream to keep you whole when I myself am a clay Buddha, dissolving as I try to ford the river. May the Goddess of Mercy protect you."

"I know, in my heart, Fourth Brother will not be coming back to us," a sister said to Nainai after Baba's departure.

Baba returned to Xinmin to pack. An undeniable intent had taken shape, a plan that had grown as silently as moss: he would walk south—there were no more trains journeying south of the Great Wall. He would head for territory held firmly in the hands of the Central Government, where surely there would be peace. Perhaps in Beiping he would still have an opportunity to attend university.

The only family members shuffling around in the dim, silent House of Yang—blind and gap-toothed from the missing windows and doors—were kindly, artless Third Brother and his wife.

Third Brother, Baba's elder by a year, always accepted guidance from Baba.

"Do not join the army, my brother, whatever you do—neither the Nationalist nor the Communist. They are equally evil," said Baba. "The maze of Shenyang is not for you. Take my sister-in-law with you to the countryside and seek shelter with the peasants. There will certainly be food in the countryside.

"Who cares which army wins, which party emerges to rule. Stay alive. There is no greater triumph than staying alive one more day."

A relentless hunger had come to Manchuria, and my father was reversing the steps of the Great Progenitor who had arrived to settle upon this land, escaping the hunger in his own time.

One May morning in 1947, when the sorghum was just waist high, Baba began his journey upon a narrow wagon lane, winding through the dunes crowned by stubbles of willows.

Beyond the dunes of sand deposited by the river Liu, where would the mute and motionless road, the long road that would blister and bleed his feet, ultimately lead him? Not even his dreams whisper of the path, thousands of li long, that would zigzag like a dragon down the length of China and across the sea. No, Baba at eighteen could not have imagined an absence of thirty-two years from beneath the Manchurian sky.

But he could certainly envision this: that the road would cleave him from the familiar, each step expanding the distance between himself and Old Granddaddy Hill in Shantuozi, where eight generations of the Yang Clan had lived and prospered. He could only trust that Guanyin, the goddess in whose protective powers his mother believed so fervently, would keep watch over them all.

It is said that a man without his family is but a *guhun yegui*—a solitary ghost, a savage spirit: a man of no value. But I must tell you, Baba will not travel alone, for this is not his maiden voyage. He is journeying forth upon a road of memory, and I, his daughter, will be with him, riding high upon his shoulders to dream the landscape of China, unrolling like a great, long painted scroll.

ACKNOWLEDGMENTS

"If this book were a painted paper kite," Baba says, "then it has taken the breaths of many people to send it into the sky. If this book began as a mere spark, then it has taken many people, each bringing a twig, a branch, to feed the flame." To you, generous souls, a thousand *xie-xie*.

Mrs. James R. Lilley, first and foremost. Thank you. Forever, xie-xie. From across the seas you filled me with hope. Life has not been the same since. Wishing you and the Ambassador a long, beautiful life together.

Incredible Amy Tan, angel of the highest order. It is my greatest joy and luck to have received your blessing. I wish you days of inspiration and peace, rolling out one after another in an endless stream.

Sue Yung Li, for your generous heart. You stopped and gave a hand to a stranger.

Sandra Dijkstra, literary protector: omniscient, omnipresent. Best in the West; best of the best. With love and great respect. Professor Bram Dijkstra, thank you for taking care of Sandy when she works longer than she should for all of her authors.

Bill Messing, faithful friend of my rainy Beijing days. Your words of comfort carry me to this day. May life bring you, Sophie, and Tina the very best.

Patti Compton, director of Gallery Who's Who in Art, Monterey, California. Cheerleader, cheer-giver whose tireless efforts supplied this artist with paints, paper, and wisdom.

Judie Telfer, solid gold, who said "There are stories in your paintings" and set me to face the first blank sheet of paper. Thank you for the heavenly walks and heartening talks at Point Lobos.

My Carmel teachers who said "Never forget your art!": Nancy Johnson, Ken Wiese, Joe Broadman, William F. Stone, Jr. Three more from home who challenged and encouraged: the great Buzz Rainer, Wally LeValley, and Dr. Kenneth Bullock. You made all the difference in the world to a girl in braids.

To the family of people at Harcourt Brace & Company, my publishing home, shaken by a temblor in January of 1994. Thank you for steering your authors and their beloved children to safety first. May life always steer you toward beautiful, lofty things:

Claire Wachtel—senior editor, forthright friend, godmother of this book—"I will not forsake you," you said to me. I will never forget you. You are a brilliant combination of guidance and freedom; your clear, concise editorial comments sparked my understanding and were vital to shaping this book into a harmonious whole. It is a privilege, an honor, and a miracle of meeting to work with you. Love always to you, Rachel, and Paul.

Leigh Haber—Geoffrey and Sam's wonderful, genuine mom—appreciation from deep within my heart for your concern and support.

Alane Mason and Dori Weintraub, reassuring voices clear on the other side of the country. Thank you for taking me under your expansive wings during uncertain days. I am more grateful than you will know.

Lisa Peters, Vaughn Andrews, and Warren Wallerstein, for the artistry and painstaking care that give body to the spirit. Thank you for a stunning book.

Deborah D. Warren, for sending this child out into the world with good directions.

Ted Lee, Ruth Greenstein, Sheri Abramson, and Celia Wren for the tens of thousands of critical, unseen, unsung things you do.

Rubin Pfeffer, president, who has enthusiastically supported this project from the first. May your house always prosper.

Laning Yang—supreme optimist, my teacher, my Buddha, my dearest mother—thank you for spiritual sustenance, and for the endless hours you sat by, listening and correcting as I stumbled through the Chinese classics, tome by tome. Mama, you did not lose faith in me during the tortuous, darkest years. Your faith was everything. EVERYTHING.

And finally, Joseph Yang, mentor, father, and sometime sparring partner: thank you for my stubborn Manchurian streak which allows no defeat. Thank you for bringing me to America, riding high upon your shoulders. I thought you had come to this country with empty pockets. Little did I know they were jingling with stories—my inheritance.

Thank you, Baba and Mama, for the breath of life.

—BXY

March 8, 1994

The Patriarch at seventy-two years of age